Letters to an Atheist

by
Nancy Wansbrough

OT God / NT God.

see
pgs
20
28
70

99

LETTERS
TO AN ATHEIST

NANCY WANSBROUGH

1988
CHURCHMAN PUBLISHING
Worthing and Folkestone

LETTERS TO AN ATHEIST
by
Nancy Wansbrough
was first published in 1988
by
CHURCHMAN PUBLISHING LIMITED
117 Broomfield Avenue,
Worthing,
West Sussex.
BN14 7SF.

Publisher: E. Peter Smith
and Distributed to the Book Trade
by
BAILEY BOOK DISTRIBUTION LIMITED
Warner House,
Wear Bay Road,
Folkestone,
Kent.
CT19 6PH.

ISBN 1 8509 3 085 6

Printed and bound in Great Britain by
Whitstable Litho Printers Limited, Whitstable, Kent.

To Bunch, who died on April 25th 1986.

TABLE OF CONTENTS

Acknowledgments

I must first offer my warmest thanks to Eric Sams, who agreed to be written to, and what is more, wrote back, with telling effect.

I owe a debt of deep gratitude to my tutors at the South London Christian Studies Centre, Canon Leslie Houlden of King's College, London, and the Reverend Alan Race, Director of Studies of the Southwark Ordination Course. Despite initial misgivings, they consented to the inclusion of their off-the-cuff comments on my essays, never of course intended for publication. Thus while providing necessary corrections of fact they have helped to convey the flavour of the experience I am reporting: I am still amazed at the expenditure of so much time and trouble on us evening class mature students. Errors that may remain are of course my responsibility.

May I thank Peggy Pyke-Lees for her forthright criticism and encouragement, and also Mary Wright, friend and secretary of many years, who typed the manuscript.

LETTERS TO AN ATHEIST

INTRODUCTION

'It had to be the Bishop of Durham who gave expression to the Church's unease. It was he who broke with the convention of discretion about doctrine, *by saying what many Bishops privately say, and what a generation of clergy have learned in their theological colleges,* that the virgin birth and similar articles of the faith are not literally true.'

Clifford Longley, Times Religious Correspondent
TIMES, September 25th 1984.

Well, what *has* a generation of clergy learned in their theological colleges that has not trickled through to us in the pews; nor apparently, to judge by the outcry, to all the clergy themselves?

What do modern Biblical scholars say? Do they all say the same thing? Why haven't we been told? What difference does it make anyhow?

In point of fact, I had already determined to satisfy my own curiosity on this score months before the Bishop of Durham controversies erupted. They confirmed my resolve. After some fishing about, I found myself, in September 1984, enrolled in an Extra-mural Theology Diploma Course of London University, for a course of 24 lectures on the New Testament by Canon J. L. Houlden, M.A., Senior Lecturer in New Testament Studies at King's College, Strand. About half of the students were training for the stipendiary and non-stipendiary ministry of the Church. The remainder, including a number of teachers, had other objectives.

My own reasons for taking this course were: first, to go back to the first century, in highly critical vein, and find out what modern Biblical scholarship (i.e. the Bishop of Durham amongst others) can tell the ordinary non-theologian about how Christianity began. What is historical fact? What is myth? If the first chapter of Genesis is myth, which is surely no longer disputed except in the most extreme fundamentalist outposts, how far may the process go?

Secondly, to aim to discover how it can come about that two old friends, of the same twentieth century Oxbridge culture, can hold totally opposing views on the validity of the Christian faith and yet arrive at a close consensus on operational values.

And thirdly, to see what light the course throws on two major current preoccupations — viz. the relation between religion and science today in the era of post-Einstein physics and quantum mechanics; and the relation of Christianity to the other major world faiths.

'And that', said another old friend to whom I presented this programme, 'should just about wrap it up. You're not short on optimism, are you?' But of course we both knew that even if these mighty questions were susceptible to being wrapped up, the present writer was not the one to do it. Theologians, physicists and historians, men and women who have devoted a life-time to the consideration of these matters, are the people for that if anyone. But this presents a further problem in addition to the inherent difficulty of the subject matter, namely, the specialisation of modern academic disciplines. Stranded in their jargon and all but choked by the rarity of the intellectual air they breathe, these experts are barely intelligible to the rest of us. Momentous discoveries are just not getting through. It struck me that what was needed was an interpreter, someone willing and able to look up 'syncretism' and 'soteriology' in the Oxford English Dictionary but in other respects entirely ordinary. I thought I might do for the job. And while I grappled like any young student with the lectures and essays of an academic course, I thought it would be interesting to write about it to the atheist old friend of the Oxbridge culture, relaying discoveries and impressions as one went along — and dealing with the backlash.

This is what happened.

YEAR I

26 September 1984

Dear Nancy,

Well, good luck!

By October, I note, you'll already be an enrolled *domina* at Southwark. Is it St. Mary Overy, did you say, where they buried Shakespeare's brother with a tolling of the great bell in the forenoon? There too lived, and lie, Beaumont and Fletcher; and in their death they were not divided though whether they are still collaborating seems decidedly more dubious to me. University Extension sounds about right too, like Jacob's ladder, pitched between Heaven and London Bridge . . .

Love E.

2nd October 1984

My dear E,

Many thanks for your latest missive.

Yes, I am now a fully paid-up, turned up, Diploma-type student at the South London Christian Studies Centre, 27 Blackfriars Road just over the Bridge. Christchurch, rebuilt after bombing, not St. Mary Overy (which I've never heard of) with all these historic associations you give. A rather prosaic setting architecturally, and by no means custom-built to house four full size extra-mural classes simultaneously. So they have one class in the church itself, one in the church hall, another upstairs in a genuine classroom, raked but unlovely, and a fourth, ours, in another nondescript, office-like appendage. There is a busy little canteen where you can get coffee and sandwiches, and a 5.30p.m. Eucharist every Thursday. The night I go there are some hundred people milling about, meeting each other, fixing this and that, eating, drinking, gossiping and perusing the noticeboard. This last emphasises what a peripheral student I shall be, because people training for any sort of ministry have

1

various weekends and extra meetings in addition to the formal courses. Must remember this.

Our class numbers 25, I think. 15 women and 10 men, a typically nondescript assorted careworn lot. One or two beards and anoraks to offset the suits and tweed jackets. A number of teachers, and a number of distinctly pretty younger women, with nice firm voices. One such gave me a lift to Waterloo afterwards, in her low-slung sports car, being *en route* for Knightsbridge, where she explained, being married to a merchant banker, she was due at a dinner party after our lecture. This was not the sort of fellow-student I had expected.

The class started with a few preliminaries and to my amazement I heard myself volunteering to be class librarian. No one else offered, and after all, they are mostly working. Our Tutor is Canon Houlden of King's College and very experienced and expert I found him. Author of several books and reputed to be sound though capable of upsetting people. So far so good.

As to the content, it was very much a case of scene setting in time, place and chronology in very broad sweeps. Why is it, I wonder, that one never hears it mentioned that the Pauline Epistles preceded the Gospels? And the other thing that strikes one is that interpretation was built in from the very start. The method of the compilation of the Gospels (and compilation seems the *mot juste*) makes it evident that there was an element of choice and selection of stories from the word go. New Testament scholarship seems to preclude any possibility of abstract 'givenness'. And yet there is this vast segment of Christendom in the shape of the Fundamentalists who believe precisely in that. Among them the young man who wrote that erudite study of C.S. Lewis's view of the Scriptures. It matters not to him that C.S. Lewis never put forward a view of the nature of the Scriptures; he just works it out from first principles. A study of inerrancy. Does this not fill you with alarm as it does me? Whatever Christianity turns out to be or not to be, surely to goodness it cannot rest on overturning logic and scholarship. We are after all a post-Galileo society. Everyone, including the most devoted, is bidden in hymn and collect to use their minds as well as their hearts.

2

I find that St. Mary Overy is Southwark Cathedral, which sounds much duller.

Love Nancy

8th October 1984

Dear Nancy,

Many thanks for yours. Great excitement. No, I didn't know that Paul was prior. What's the evidence, I wonder? I've discovered that scholars will say and believe absolutely anything. If the Epistles came first, isn't that rather damaging? How come that Paul doesn't mention (i.e. didn't know about) a great many rather significant events? I'd always rather suspected that he made up his own Jesus ad lib: the two figures seem to differ as much from each other (i.e. in Epistles and Gospels) as the Gods of the Old and New Testament.

Love E.

28th October 1984

My dear E,

Great excitement as you say, about the dating of the Epistles and Gospels, and the Epistles, much to the astonishment of both of us, coming first. In fact, on my part, great excitement about the whole enterprise. Leslie Houlden is a brilliant lecturer (and I've heard a few). I find he was Chaplain of Trinity, Oxford before becoming Head of Cuddesdon (Church of England Theological College near Oxford). Now he is King's College, London, a theologian of the liberal kind. From the point of view of what I was looking for, couldn't be better.

After which preamble, the chronology of the New Testament. You say 'Is there one single simple sane *reason* for giving Paul priority?' No. There seem to be a whole string of reasons or rather deductions, but the surprising thing is that all the scholars seem to agree within a year or two. I have in front of me now — not yet read —

Paul — by Günther Bornkamm 1971 (tr)
Pauline Christianity — John Ziesler 1983
How to read the N.T. — Etienne Charpentier 1981

3

They all agree in placing Paul's death, perhaps in the Nero persecution, at anything between AD 60 and AD 67, which is before the fall of Jerusalem in AD 70 and one reason why he didn't mention it! And while we're about it, the other main reason is that the epistles were not that sort of communication. They were not modern histories — any more than the gospels were biographies of Christ in the modern sense.

But back to dating evidence. According to Bornkamm, writing from Heidelberg in 1969, all Pauline chronology is deduced from Acts 18:12 which says 'But when Gallio was proconsul of Achaia'.

Bornkamm writes 'On the basis of an inscription found at Delphi, his period of office as proconsul of Achaia can be calculated as being from the spring of 51 to the spring of 52 (less probably 52-53). All further relative dating has to be conjectured by calculation both forward and backward from this point . . .' (p.xi). He then sets out a table of such calculated dates. Paul's conversion is put at c. AD 32, and his first epistle, I Thessalonians at AD 51. Ziesler and Charpentier substantially agree.

You say you have been looking at the evidence. Where, I wonder? I'm not sure when all this modern N.T. scholarship started — I must ask — but I have the impression that it's relatively recently that it has concentrated attention on the type of recipients, and types of communities, and the purposes they serve, to which both epistles and gospels were addressed: and when you do that, you get a much more rounded, comprehensible picture.

I enclose a copy of my first essay to show what I have found out.

Love Nancy

23.X.84

4

How did the New Testament come into existence as a collection of authoritative writings?

One answer to the question posed may be made as follows:

The New Testament came into existence as a collection of authoritative writings in response to a felt need, or, rather, a succession of felt needs, in a world of cause and effect; the point being that we owe its canonicity to happenings which constitute the very reverse of sudden divine intervention. If the scriptures are indeed the word of God, they can simultaneously carry a perfectly rational human explanation. Why not?

The felt need in this case was the need to look after the churches. Robert Grant in his *'Historical Introduction to the N.T.'* makes this point clearly.[1] Paul and the writers of the other letters were the first to whom this became apparent, quite possibly well within twenty five years of the crucifixion, if the dating of I. Thessalonians at c. AD 51 is accepted. The church communities founded in the first headlong flush of enthusiasm were now in need, not only of encouragement and admonition, but of theological interpretation of the experiences that both they and their founder had undergone. By the time the second generation of Christians grew up, the need was to document the outstanding features in the life of Jesus for the benefit of those who could not have known him. Hence the Gospels.

Of course the process of consolidation was gradual. So far as the Jews were concerned, the particular and strange nature of Jesus's messiahship took time to sink in). (J.L.H. But the first converts were Jews and for most, it didn't ever sink in). So far as the Gentiles living far beyond Judaea were concerned (particularly after the fall of Jerusalem in AD 70) the revolutionary implications of their recruitment, though tackled head-on by Paul, (J.L.H. dead by 70!) also became only gradually apparent. In fact they continued to be resisted for many years.

This brief essay into interpretation may account for the Gospels and the Epistles. But the Book of Revelation is an entirely different proposition from which the student coming fresh to these studies recoils. One wonders (as indeed did certain early thinkers) whether some mistake has not been made, especially on recalling to what wrong-headed use the juggling

5

with signs and numbers has subsequently been put by fringe sects. What has to be said is that the need for scholarly understanding of alien thought processes is here particularly great. (J.L.H. Its code of images would be intelligible to someone reared on Ezekiel and Daniel). Much marrying of cultures over time and space has to take place if Revelation is to make sense in the western twentieth century. Yet here it is, enshrined in the canon.

All this is not intended to suggest that the formation of the New Testament over three hundred years, to its consolidation by Athanasius c. 367 (J.L.H. Ath. simply first gives the list *exactly* as now) proceeded without hiccups. Nor that the exclusion of impeccable non-canonical writings can be entirely satisfactorily explained, whatever may be said of those ultimately included. Nor that the data are adequate for historical certainty without conjecture.

The data

Take first the available texts. Jesus himself wrote nothing (except, as Etienne Charpentier mentions, on one occasion in the sand). The earliest texts available are all in Greek, so we have no written legacy of the very earliest church communities before the wider Greek-speaking world became involved. It is true that some scholars have thought that the first texts may have been in Aramaic, but the evidence is unsubstantiated; certainly nothing remains.

Nor do we have the originals of the Greek texts. What we have are copies, and copies of copies of the originals in considerable profusion, in scroll and papyrus, or codex form. And what we in this country possess, due to the collecting passion of our forbears, is the earliest extant manuscript of any part of the New Testament. In the John Rylands Library in Manchester is a fragment of John, Chapter 18, recovered in Egypt and now dated by scholars at c. AD 130. Its existence at this site proved that copies of the scriptures were already going the rounds of the churches far beyond Palestine at that date.[2]

However, these early texts have been found suspect in many minor particulars. Discrepancies such as for the ending of Mark have been pointed out: later interpolations detected: variants galore between the many mss. At the end of the day, what with

6

all these imperfections and the large part played by conjecture in textual criticism, the impression is given that it remains a *chancy* business. (J.L.H. Yes, within fairly strict limits). And yet the main theme of the risen Christ comes through as it has come through for twenty centuries.

As to the chronology of the basic textual data, it may be useful to set out the agreed framework within which more detailed discussion may take place.

1. End of second century, Alexandrian 'recension' or reconciliation of discrepancies found in different manuscripts. (Alexandria in this period was a major Hellenestic and Jewish cultural centre).

2. Translation from the Greek into Latin (c. 170) Syriac and Coptic. (Early Syriac and Coptic mss. were subsequently to prove of much value).

3. Bodmer papyrus fragment giving 14 chapters of John c. AD 200. Found in Egypt.

4. Three Chester Beatty papyri, giving passages from the Gospels, Paul and Revelation. c. AD 250.

5. Codex Vaticanus and Codex Siniaticus, written on parchment, date from the mid-fourth century. Athanasius consolidation is dated c. 367.[3] (J.L.H. Athanasius is important for the *list* of books not the text itself).

It is also worth compiling by way of background information a further list of central figures whose influence on the formation of the N.T. would repay further study should the translations all be available and time permit. Such a list would include

(1) Marcion (c. 140) a Christian bishop of Asia Minor who found the God of the Old Testament barbarous and quite different from the God of the New Testament; and who therefore jettisoned the O.T. and compiled a *new testament* consisting of the letters of Paul and an expurgated Luke (J.L.H. *Perhaps* the first to do so).

(2) Papias of Hierapolis, from whose fragmentary writings deductions have been made regarding the origin of Mark's gospel (early 2nd century).

7

(3) Tatian (160 AD) who dovetailed the four gospels into one *Diatessaron,* a single version which was used for centuries in Syria.

(4) Irenaeus, the *French* bishop who was the first to countenance the diversity of the four gospels, and who appears to have written extensively on the epistles, c. 180 AD. (J.L.H. Yes. Though from Asia Minor. And he accepted 4 gospels).

(5) Eusebius of Casearea, Bishop, early fourth century, who attempted a canonical classification under the headings: acknowledged: disputed: spurious. (Acknowledged were the four gospels, Acts, fourteen epistles of Paul including Hebrews, I John, I Peter, Revelation. Among those categorised as spurious were the Acts of Paul, the Shepherd of Hermas, the Apocalypse of Peter, the Epistle of Barnabas and the Didache. James, Jude II Peter and II John were disputed). He was referred to by Athanasius, and appears to have made use of certain valid critical techniques. (J.L.H. There's the early 3rd century so-called Muratorian Canon, giving the list accepted in Rome: Gospels, Paul plus a few other Letters (*not* Hebrews)).

After extensive preliminaries the crunch question remains: what are the canonical criteria? If a case can perhaps be made for the eventual inclusion of the canonical writings on the grounds of human necessity, would such a thesis imply that the excluded writings are somehow less important for a proper understanding of right doctrine? Or for proper pastoral care of the young churches?

Yes and No. To begin with, modern tools of analysis and measurement, however indispensable in certain spheres, are simply unsuitable for dealing with general questions of this sort in which value judgments cannot but predominate. We get nowhere if we ask, for example:

1. Whether the non-canonical collected writings of Ignatius of Antioch contain *less* of the Christian message than Paul's letter to Philemon? or

2. How the account of the martyrdom of Polycarp also non-

canonical can have *less* claim on our attention than, say, Jude?

To pursue this line of thought clearly leads to absurdity. But it also points to inclusion/exclusion criteria which seems to stand up to investigation and provide an extension of the rather too ingeneous 'human need' thesis. These criteria are earliness; apostolicity (connected but not identical); orthodoxy; authenticity and church usage over a long period.

The criterion of earliness reflects the desire of the post-apostolic generations to get as close to possible to the Founder of their faith. The stories of the martyrs, however shining, represent a different genre, reflect a different need. The test of apostolicity has been well worked through by scholars: of course the apostles were early, none earlier, but they were also chosen by Christ. Orthodoxy, wrote Robert Grant, (was used) . . . 'not in a rigid sense but in the sense than most of the apocryphal documents had special axes to grind, axes different from those ground in the central "New Testament writings".[4] As to authenticity, this became important at a surprisingly early stage and was the concern of many of the early church fathers just mentioned. (J.L.H. Even though they often got it wrong!). To quote Grant yet again: "Towards the end of the second century it was recognised that Hermas, for example, lived long after New Testament times, and that the 'Acts of Paul' had been composed not as history but as edifying fiction."[5] Church usage, the last of the criteria suggested, comes nearest to the simple 'need' criterion first identified: Prolonged church usage surely implied, in any event in the first crucial centuries, the satisfaction of deep-seated need. Would the liturgists agree?

26th October 1984

Dear Nancy,

Such a good essay. Of course the logic of pragmatism (once it is pointed out) requires that the first documents are circular instructions and the like, followed by background notes, policy statements, etc. So Epistles preceded Gospels, and what's more the categories are conceptually quite separate, because serving wholly distinct purposes. All this implies, interestingly, a pre-existing private office (with, as you might call them, *ministers*) and some sort of secretariat. What was the likeliest nexus and focus, I wonder? How about Jesus's brother?

I liked the reminder about the writing in the sand. The same is said of Socrates. I suppose the Levantine deserts were like vast unbroken sheets of paper, written on only by the wind. At least Shakespeare, son of a smallholder and stock farmer, had sheepskin not parchment. And one could always pick up a quill or two (literally); dirt cheap. And what were the scriptures written on, in and with, I wonder? Why didn't they *all* speak Greek, incidentally, from the beginning? Who needs Aramaic? Might not Jesus himself as an educated person (and indeed infant prodigy) have spoken some Greek?

I very much liked too the marshalling of data in orderly sequence, as an essential preliminary, without preconception. I'm not sure though that *Church usage* is much of a criterion. I see you place it last in your list.

I enjoyed too the forthright denunciation of Revelations as lunatic ravings. I think its author must have been a Baconian.

Love E.

16th November 1984

My dear E,

Lovely to see you the other day and hear how the great work has progressed.

But may I go back to your letter of October 8th, when we were both thunderstruck by the information that Paul came chronologically before the Gospels?

I was so thunderstruck that I wondered how widely disseminated this information is. Could it be that just you and I have failed to keep up with the onward march of knowledge in this regard?

So I conducted a straw poll among the members of our local choir busily practising the Duruflé Requiem (lovely!). I asked our astonished conductor if I might, mounted the rostrum, and discovered on a show of hands that out of 18, 11 thought — had

10

never questioned — that Gospels preceded Epistles; but 7 knew the reverse. Mind you, the composition of our choir makes us representative of nobody but our sweet selves. And the fact that we gather year after year to conquer Mass after Passion after Requiem (to be sung eventually with young professional soloists and all our fellow Festival choirs), tells its own story. But it was surprising that as many as 7 of us were thus informed, I thought.

The chronology aspect came in my last essay: as to Paul's place in the scheme of things, I find you are not alone in thinking about him as you do. The extreme view is that it was really Paul that, so to speak, invented Christianity, almost independently of Jesus himself. But I have a feeling we shall be hearing more about this from Leslie Houlden when we get to the Gospels. Not that one wants to dish up one's lecture notes; but the temptation is strong, as from a background of great erudition he does produce a very clear-sighted view, while taking care to give both sides if it's disputed or speculative.

What I want to do now, if you can bear it, is to try out on you my next essay *"Discuss Paul's doctrine of justification: what did he mean by it?"* If my stamina holds out, I long to do a block-buster on this (and collect more that one 'unit' — you see how one's mind works when plunged back into the world of marks and exams?). But also for two better reasons:

(1) Because the subject is so immense and

(2) Because it would help define, with greater accuracy, our own respective positions. I continue to be foxed trying to pinpoint the difference. We see eye to eye on so much: yet you call yourself an atheist (you said humanist earlier. What's the difference? There's an essay for *you*) and I a Christian, in the direct line, as it now strikes me, from Paul Romans 1-8 and of course with all the usual disclaimers of humility.

Discuss Paul's doctrine of justification

I.   *Language*

I think I've chosen the wrong essay. One really ought to know Greek. Justification is not the sort of word you use twice before breakfast and it seems to me essential to get

11

the hang of it in the original to start with. (For language is central to the understanding of ideas. More: what is an idea without language, or language without an idea? "How do I know what I think till I see what I say?" But this is meant to be about Paul, not Wittgenstein or Benedetto Croce).

Anyhow: I've been wrestling with a Cruden's concordance and a Greek testament, and John Robinson himself wrestling with Romans[6], and it looks very much as if *Justification* and *Righteousness* are almost the same word, *dikaiosunē* but I can't be too sure because I don't know the endings and it may only be the root. (J.L.H. *dikaiosunē* is both the quality and the activity that acquits or justifies i.e. it is, normally, seen as virtue in action — God, as 'right', makes 'right' e.g. Rom. 1.16f. There is a related noun that means the abstract noun. 'justification', *dikaiōsis*.) What is certain is that the concept of both words is grounded in the Old Testament and Jewish law and use in the lawcourts, and that it carries an implication of acquittal or vindication. I've looked up two Old Testament passages to see. Exodus 23, 7 "Keep far from a false charge, and do not slay the innocent and righteous, for I will not *justify* the wicked" says the Authorised Version. The RSV (Revised Standard Version) has "I will not *acquit* the wicked". Again, Deut. 25.1. "If there is a dispute between men, and they come into court, and the judges decide between them "they shall *justify* the righteous and condemn the wicked" (A.V.), or "*acquit*(ting) the innocent and condemn(ing) the guilty." (R.S.V.)

Turning to the N.T. I looked up a short passage for the sake of simplicity, Romans 5.1. in a number of different renderings, e.g. A.V., R.S.V., Wand, Philiips, New English Bible, Good News[7]. All give *justified* even including Phillips with his free paraphrasing, except two. Bishop Wand has.

> "Since then we have been *acquitted* on the score of faith, let us be at peace with God through our Lord Jesus Christ"

(J.L.H. The only trouble with 'acquit' is its English

12

connotations of rather formal cold legal procedures and its negative 'feel': it is a letting off — no more: 'put right' gets the creative aspect in — and that is certainly there in the biblical usage).

And the translation of the Good News, clumsily it must be admitted, "Now that we have been *put right with* God through faith, we have peace with God through Jesus Christ our Lord". Considering the upshot of this short exercise, it would appear that if one were to line up the meanings of the word *justify* along a spectrum, then Wand brings out the old tight legalistic right, the Good News the free-wheeling left. The idea of "putting people right with God" is the interpretation currently in favour.

II. *Paul's doctrine*
Paul's doctrine of justification must be well known to anyone who has been to a communion service, or to a Catholic Mass, or indeed who has sung one of the great Latin masses; for they are built upon it. God requires not that one keeps a set of rules, but that one *believes in* Christ, from which all sorts of consequences flow. (J.L.H. Yet this needs 'interpreting!' note it's, in Paul, the opposite of operating by works.) In essence it is as simple as that. The complications set in as one attempts to elucidate the tortuous passages in which Paul proclaims this gospel to the gentiles and to the world while struggling with his own inborn, still persistent, still inescapable Jewishness. With the eye of logic (which he is not short of), he perceives the total incompatibility of Jewish Law and Christian faith. But it is the eye of a Jew, a top-educated Jew, to whom Jewish historical illustrations spring most readily to mind, and to whom it is still important to reconcile the Old Testament with the New (J.L.H. I suppose the N.T. was not there for P!). The tension lies within Paul himself. Of course, as you will see, I have been over-simplifying. I think I had better therefore indicate one or two passages where Paul expresses his thought most fully, Romans 1-8 and Galatians. This will introduce the complications. To save you looking them up, here is one of the best translations of a *locus classicus* Romans 3. 21-26.

13

But now God's way of putting people right with himself has been revealed. It has nothing to do with law, even though the law of Moses and the prophets gave their witness to it. God puts people right through their faith in Jesus Christ. God does this to all who believe in Christ, because there is no difference at all; everyone has sinned and is far away from God's saving presence

But by the free gift of God's grace all are put right with him through Christ Jesus who sets them free (Good News).

This is Paul the theologian, elaborating a thesis in a relatively settled situation and I confess it doesn't say much to me. A much more exciting picture of the doctrine in action, so to speak, comes in Galatians. Evidently the Church of Galatia (wherever that may be — nobody knows) (J.L.H. Well we know near enough!) had been got at by Jewish Christians of some description, who were insisting that in order to be proper Christians, it was necessary to undergo circumcision as well as baptism, and obey the Mosaic Law as well. Paul works himself into a white hot fury as he writes to upbraid them.

"O foolish Galatians! Who has bewitched you? . . . Let me ask you only this: Did you receive the Spirit by works of the law, or by hearing with faith? Are you so foolish? etc., etc." (Gal. 3.1).

"For in Christ Jesus neither circumcision nor uncircumcision is of any avail, but faith working through love. You were running well, who hindered you from obeying the truth?" (Gal. 5.6).

"I wish that the people who are upsetting you would go all the way: Let them go and castrate themselves!" (Gal. 5.12.).

As to the meaning of 'grace' in this context, the kind of elusive theologicial concept which I suspect to be inadmissible to a humanist, Morna Hooker (Lady Margaret Professor of Divinity at Cambridge) is particularly good.[8]

The law having failed to produce the right relationship, it is only entry into the spirit of Christ (J.L.H. It's a matter of God's gift or initiative), sacrifice, expiation and all, that 'justifies' the seeker. Further, the spirit is God-given, something akin to Shakespearean mercy (SNW not Hooker) and cannot be achieved by self-motivation, striving, or the accomplishment of good works. And when all this occurs, x (= Paul or mankind) freed from sin enters into this right relationship with God the father so that he too may call him *Abba*.

So far, so good. Now come the complications.

III. *The Jewish elements*
At least five elements of Jewish thought form an integral part of Paul's argument — circumcision: Abraham: the curse of crucifixion: sacrifice and expiation: the End; and in order to grasp Paul's own thinking in its entirety, it strikes me (again) as essential to attempt to understand these.

i) *Circumcision*
It came as quite a shock to realise that I had no idea why the Jews set such store on the rite of circumcision and still do. How deficient one's education is. Do you know?

Well, it is nothing less than the command of God to seal his original covenant with Abraham and his descendants the Jewish people, so no wonder. The whole episode comes in Genesis 17. It reads:

> "And God said to Abraham, 'As for you, you shall keep my covenant, you and your descendants after you throughout their generations. This is my covenenant . . . : Every male among you shall be circumcised . . . and it shall be a sign of the covenant between me and you . . . Any uncircumcised male who is not circumcised in the flesh of his foreskin shall be cut off from his people: he has broken my covenant" (R.S.V.)

I repeat: this is powerful stuff and no wonder Paul (safely circumcised himself) had such trouble with it.

15

ii) *Abraham*
He has particular trouble in relation to Abraham, circumcised as above and hoping against hope to become as promised, and at the age of 99, the father of many nations. (Genesis 15. Romans 4.) It took all Paul's skills as debater, if not casuist, to point out as it were the small print in the Genesis story: that faith was reckoned to Abraham as righteousness not after, but before he was circumcised (Gen. 15.6). One can sense that it was because of his own Jewishness that Paul found it necessary thus elaborately to unravel this ancient, basic, myth.

iii) *Sacrifice and expiation*
In the densely packed passage already quoted as a description of the Pauline doctrine — Romans 3.21-26 — Christ's death is seen as expiation for sin. As Morna Hooker wrote:

> "It was an obvious image for Paul to use, since the blood of the sin-offering was intended to remove the sins of those who had infringed the law: far more effective . . . the death of Christ now achieved what the law was incapable of doing, and made reconciliation between God and man possible."[9]

iv) *The curse of crucifixion*
Relatively, this is a smaller point, but illustrative of how Paul's mind works. Apparently the Law announced that anyone who was hanged on a tree was under a curse. Morna Hooker points out that God, by raising Christ from the dead, gives notice of his divine approval which thus overrides the curse of the Law (*Pauline Pieces*, p. 40). (J.L.H. This aspect was one that, I think, *forced* P. to see the Law as now redundant — Christ had come under its curse and so, somehow, transcended it — see Rom 10.4.)

v) *The end*
Finally, there is the all-pervading eschatological climate, stemming from the Books of Daniel and Ezekiel, about which I know nothing, and which I am more than prepared to leave in the laps of the professional theologians. But do look up, if you have time I Corinthians 6. In it Paul chides

the brethren for going to law against each other, to be tried by outsiders at that, when they will shortly themselves be called upon to judge the angels! (J.L.H. Yes, in Christ, God has brought the 'things of the End' already into the present — they are already in train and moving towards their conclusion.)

vi) *After justification what then?*
The above are a few thoughts, and no block-buster, set down with really genuine diffidence. From the point of view of accuracy no doubt I'd have done better to extract even larger chunks than I have from the numerous excellent commentators. But if we are to have any sort of dialogue, I must 'internalise', in the hideous jargon of the sociologists, and this is the result. Lots is omitted such as the interesting question whether Paul, writing in the first person singular, was referring to himself or to the wider world. From the practical point of view, I can't see that it matters.[10]

Whoever it is, Paul, you or *I* that goes through the justification process, he arrives at what? Salvation. Now the fact of the matter is, nobody these days cares a tuppenny rap about salvation. The Concise Oxford Dictionary gives "Saving of the soul: deliverance from sin and its consequences and admission to heaven brought about by Christ", conveying a wholly egotistical and I would have thought counter-productive objective. Some aspects of Marxism, the CND, World Wildlife Fund and the ecological movements present to this generation a much more acceptable altruism, and call forth equal degrees of devotion.

I understand we have Luther to thank for this state of affairs: the tortured introspective Western conscience and all that. Leslie Houlden finds that Romans 9-11 absolves Paul from the charge of self-centredness by indicating his concern for the social groupings of the day — Israel and the Gentiles *en bloc*. This is not wholly clear to me.

But perhaps we need look no further than back to Paul himself and the fruits of the spirit: proclaimed in such beautiful language too.[11] Cannot these be emphasised more

17

often to supplant that wretched salvation?

(J.L.H. Even apart from his 'Israel' perspective in Rom. 9-11, he sees man as brought into a corporate entity — 'body of Christ' language etc. I Cor. 12; Rom 12, i.e. 'salvation' 'well-being with God', is a shared salvation.)

23rd November 1984

My dear Nancy,

Whoa there! I can see there's much to be said for a plunge *in media res*, but I've taken my stand a very long way indeed even from the fringes, let alone the middle, of the topics now proposed. I am indeed, as you rightly suggest, quite interested in the *theological*, which ought (at least *prima facie*) to contain an element of the logical: but the *religious* means to me only religious mania. If in the beginning is the word, and the word belongs to any part of the monastic (or padded) cell or the torture chamber, then it's going to fall on not just deaf but plugged ears. This isn't at all out of any wish to be anything other than receptive and helpful: it is that I'm, both by temperament and training, utterly inimical to all the basic assumptions of the Christian faith as I understand it. I should want to begin by being shown why in this world or out of it anyone would wish, or even agree for the sake of argument, to make any such assumptions or Assumptions.

What I think about circumcision, for example, is (since you ask) that both ritual mutilation and general sanitary and dietary prescriptions in the Genesis-Leviticus vein might well have been very suitable, even necessary, for a nomadic tribe of Semites, especially in hot weather; but why any Anglo-Saxon in a more technological and hygenic age and temperate climate should be expected to take any serious account of them, even for a single second, is far beyond many plummet lines depth of anything I can fathom. I have to add, moreover, that they seem to me all too suitable for a religion of guilt, sin, redemption, blood, hellfire, flagellation and general torture all round which seems to me just a form of lunacy, and a peculiarly vicious and repugnant form at that. Even for a theist, the Genesis — O.T. notions of divine covenants and sacrifices and so forth could still

18

be horrendous blasphemies: and I as an atheist object to them strenuously on behalf of the personal deity in whom I Absolutely don't believe. One wouldn't attribute such things to a Christian dog, let alone God.

Some things I understand, or at least am always ready to try to understand; theological problems e.g. of priority, or attribution, aesthetic questions of the Bible as literature, influence, etc. But the merely religious questions devastate whole tracts of my mind like a scorched earth policy. Perhaps this is just a musico-literary critical stereotype — much the same attitude as William Empson's as described in today's TLS, I notice; he's rather against that old torture monster and Nobodaddy, the God who was *satisfied* by the crucifixion — the same God (or rather God) who at an earlier stage of his development was tickled pink by circumcision. Is this the God who *requires that one believes in Christ*? He must be off his Godhead. He must surely have noticed by now that only a tiny minority of homo sapiens from Olduvai man to the present (a million years or so and countless billions of individuals) have ever done, or even had the smallest chance of doing, anything of the kind. What in heaven's name does He think He's playing at?

And given my basic and profound antipathy to all these weird doctrines, what can I say (try as I will) to such notions as expiation by 'the blood of the sin-offering' except that they make me feel metaphysically and indeed almost physically quite sick?

Nor does Galatians help. Can one of these incidentally be the verse of which Browning wrote

> There's a great text in Galatians
> once you trip on it, entails
> twenty nine distinct damnations
> one sure, if another fails?

I'm sorry about all this: but I have to speak as I find, and I don't find any way in to the deity or the religion of sado-masochism. Where do I *begin*? Let's do it *thoroughly*.

Love E

Otterbourne

2nd December 1984

My dear E,
Goodness — I seem to have touched a nerve, which, after the
initial shock, is probably a good thing since it elicits a clear
statement of where you stand, as you say, and this has hitherto
not been evident to me. For instance, I had not understood the
great gulf fixed between theology and religion in your mind —
but surely not universally? I mean, surely theology consists in
more than attributions?

Nor had I hoisted on board that the E who is so widely read in
this field, as in so many others, and who so generously showers
upon one aids to study like Josephus, C.S. Lewis *et al*, is in
principle so deeply inimical at heart. Nor do I quite believe it.

Having said this, my last effort addressed directly to you, did I
grant you fire ahead without preliminary but this was not
through any wish to jump your gun, but simply because I was so
short of time, and am such a slow worker, that I hit upon the idea
of combining *essay* with *Letter to an Atheist* — with Leslie
Houldon's aquiescence in the unusual essay format. So far as he
was concerned, the result was β α, 2 units. So far as you are
concerned, fireworks.

Perhaps I ought to make a little clearer where it is that *I*
stand. First, I don't for one moment believe in a God who "at an
earlier stage of his development was tickled pink by
circumcision". It seems to me plain as a pikestaff (or whatever
the weapon is) that the reason for the scoundrelly character of
the God of the Old Testament is absolutely nothing to do with
God at all (if he exists) but everything to do with the primitive
character of the nomadic tribe of Israelites. This was their
perception, as different as chalk from cheese from the perception
of a C.S. Lewis.

And to go on with circumcision, I am interested, from the point
of view of scholarship, to discover how it came to predominate in
the thinking of the Jews — and why it took such a lot of
winkling out! I mean, in this matter I'm in entire agreement
with you. The thesis of my essay was that Paul is too, but that

20

old habits of thinking die hard, and Paul had still many O.T. habits of thinking cluttering up his otherwise very astute mind. And that all this is important if one is endeavouring to discover, with the aid of modern biblical scholarship (which is so *sensible*), what is the kernal of the Christian faith. Like you, I should have thought that archaic, primitive ideas of 'blood of sin-offering' which is pure O.T., could safely after 2,500 years be jettisoned altogether, otherwise than for scholarly study of antecedents.

I don't know if you are prepared to go along with the above. Nor whether it is theology or the dreaded religion. Also I can see where it leads: to a god who consists in a string of subjective perceptions. The present Reith lecturer had something to say about the place of the subjective in reality, which may be *à propos*.

love, Nancy

9th December 1984

Dear Nancy,

As to the difference in my mind between theology and religion, its roughly equivalent to the object/subject dichotomy: one studies theology, one experiences religion (or doesn't).

> The tokens that to Israel came
> to me they have not come.

I'm perfectly sure that you may not pick and choose among testaments to suit yourself. The God of Christianity is the God of the Old Testament, never doubt that. You accept or reject the package. Doesn't it strike you as perhaps the least little bit patronising to say that Paul was as it were tainted with O.T. habits of thought? He was an Old Testament Jew, surely, through and through. So was Jesus, if the Gospels are any guide. He was forever saying things like It is written (Matthew 4.6,7). I am come to fulfil the law and the prophets (5.17 7.12). Don't pray like the heathen, i.e. the goyim (6.7) don't be like those Gentiles (6.32) make the appropriate ritual offering (8.4); he thought it OK to drown the swine (presumably because they were only *pork*) (8.32) and so on: he was a synagogue teacher, a rabbi, a Jew wholly, grounded and founded in the Old Testament. What

21

you call (and I don't dissent) the archaic primitive ideas of the blood of sin offering are surely not only specifically Christian but Jesus's own ideas in his own language, from his own tradition and teaching? Redemption from sin by his blood was after all his idea (synoptic gospels: can't find it in John). I thought it was the sacred heart of the creed? I'm sorry to have to reiterate that I find it wholly repugnant and rather mad. What next: quo vadis?

Yours as ever,
E

King's College London
Faculty of Theology and Religious Studies

Nancy,

I think a great deal depends on how far one regards *historical sympathy* as part of the picture. If one is a Christian yet sensitive to critical considerations, then one is aware both of living in our culture (with its rejection of ancient taboos etc.) and of being in a tradition of faith (which has so subtly and deeply conditioned our culture). So, one feels a strong obligation to try to understand Paul in his own right, in his own context, *and* to recognise profound human issues which he discussed in terms now alien-yet-familiar (partly) to us. Even if one is a historically sensitive unbeliever, one might feel the same kind of obligation, while distancing oneself from any kind of commitment to the tradition stemming from Paul. Others will, of course, just feel Paul etc. was so 'primitive' that his stuff won't do. But, as you point out, your friend seems not to give P. the credit for having begun a process of rejection and reinterpretation of these old taboos etc. (albeit in a different idiom from our way of doing it nowadays) which has, by various routes, led to our present scepticism about them.

Leslie

10.9.84

22

Dear Nancy,

I'm awaiting, all trepidation, the latest theological cross-court volley, like Jehovah thundering out of Zion.

. . . This is anyhow just a quickie, a loin girding for the graver task of theological study. I saw a good chap on TV today who is fearful that religion may destroy the world, and calls it 'licensed insanity!' . . .

Love as ever, E

Early January 1985

Dear E,

Am desperately short of time. This is the next essay,

What problems did Paul encounter in his dealing with the Church in Corinth?

Synthesising, summarising, trying to make sense of Paul's chaotic and headlong flights of thought, one is tempted to view all his problems with the Corinthian church as ultimately reducible to one — the problem of consolidation: consolidation of his authority, consolidation of doctrine, consolidation of the rules of behaviour for daily living. There may be some advantage in such an approach. But it undermines the sheer drama and immediacy of each dilemma as it was presented to him unsynthesised and in sequence (though which sequence is not always clear). Nonetheless it provides a framework for a discussion.

Paul's authority was challenged in Corinth from at least three quarters.

There were, as always, the Jews. Paul's first visit to Corinth may be dated by reference to the proconsulship of Gallio as taking place in roughly AD 50-52, at which time Christianity (not yet so called) was still regarded as a sect within Judaism. Paul walked therefore a perpetual tight-rope with his fellow-Jews who stood watchful for any infringement of the law, or for any of Paul's periodic proclamations, unacceptable to strict

Jewry, that Jesus was the Messiah they sought. An occasion of this sort arose during this first mission: "But when Gallio was proconsul of Achaia, the Jews made a united attack upon Paul and brought him before the tribunal, saying "This man is persuading men to worship God contrary to the law". In contrast to a previous occasion, when Pontius Pilate governed and not Gallio, the plot misfired and it was upon the ruler of the synagogue, and not Paul, that the mob vented their anger. "But Gallio paid no attention to this" (Acts. 18).

(J.L.H. Acts tells of the prominence of Jews in Corinth in relation to Paul's mission there. Yet in 1 Cor. one gets very little in the way of a Jewish component either in the environment or in the Christian community. Acts may be stereotyping: a first approach to Jews is his standard pattern in describing Paul's method in each place.)

Dealing with his fellow-Jews (one has the impression) was however all in the day's work for Paul, endemic to his entire ministry. The challenges posed by the divisions within the church, and also by the arrival on the scene of the 'superlative' or 'extra-special' apostles, bearing with them letters of introduction (from Jerusalem?) may well have caused him greater anguish. (J.L.H. Yes, Jews from outside (Jerusalem?) are a problem by the time of 2 Cor.)

The unity of the young church was threatened by difficulties which came on very different levels, personal, temperamental and theological. The open quarrelling reported by 'Chloe's people' (Cor. 1.11), when one group followed Peter, another Apollos, and another Paul, is perhaps the easiest to comprehend. Factions have bedevilled all institutions since the beginning of time. In parenthesis, it is worth remarking on the part played by Apollos here. Bornkamm vigorously refutes the idea that he was himself responsible for the conditions of disruption, and indeed, if one turns up the reference to him in Acts (18:24ff), he gives the impression of a powerful but by no means arrogant intellect, quite prepared to be taken in hand by the estimable Aquila and Priscilla in order to increase his efficacy as a preacher. (J.L.H. We really know so little about Apollos.) Paul himself spoke of him more than once in straightforward terms without a hint of disapprobation (1 Cor. 1:12; 3.4-9; 16:12). In any event, these factional divisions called forth some of Paul's most imaginative and poetic teaching "I planted, Apollos watered, but God gave the increase". (1 Cor. 3:6.) What more is there to be said?

More subtle disparagement of Paul's authority came from the 'wise' in the congregation. "Jews demand signs and Greeks seek wisdom, but we preach Christ crucified, a stumbling block to Jews and folly to Gentiles." (1 Cor. 1:22f.) New Testament scholars have in recent years thrown fresh light on the meaning of 'wisdom' in this context (or rather on *one* of the meanings: for Paul switches to and fro in confusing play on the word). One meaning can be the so-called 'wisdom' of the eastern religions, no intellectual wisdom but a necromancer's initiation into dark and hidden mysteries. The city of Corinth in the first century would have provided ideal conditions for the syncretistic intrusion of such cults, sited as it was as a centre of strategic and commercial importance, its two ports facing east and west, its seafarers importing not only merchandise but pagan beliefs and practices. Nonetheless, Paul worries away at the idea of the wisdom (in its normal meaning) of man and the foolishness of God in no less than four chapters of 1 Corinthians (1-4), in passage after passage of free-thinking and back-tracking. (J.L.H. Paul-trained in technical rhetoric — able to use a term like 'wisdom' with clever paradox and ambiguity). And, again in parenthesis, there comes to this student an image of Paul in the process of dictation; thoughts flying thicker and faster than the poor amanuensis can get them down, a series of brilliant flashes on a recurring theme rather than the tidy exposition of his later critical exegesists. I once worked with a Jewish research director of great intellectual power, whose habit it was to dictate reports of considerable complexity off the top of his head, striding up and down and practically jumping out of his skin at the effort of capturing his arguments and his visions, and seeing them safely on to paper. Could Paul have been like that? But working with only one draft?

The challenge which evidently got Paul on the raw was however that delivered by the 'superlative' apostles (RSV) or 'those very special so-called apostles of yours' (Good News). Who these were precisely is not known. They came bearing letters of recommendation which Paul clearly found to be intolerable, between his missionary visits, and occasioning the fierce, scornful reproachful outpourings of II Corinthians 11; and the famous passages detailing his trials and hardships, and also his Jewish credentials; the whole a flood of self-justification of a man touchingly unsure of himself.

On the subject of the consolidation of doctrine — or perhaps rather the conduct of worship, it is not always easy to distinguish these matters from matters of unity and organisation. Doctrinally, Paul returns always to the same theme — the wisdom of man set against the foolishness of God as exemplified in Christ crucified; and the need of the young church to fasten on to this central truth and resist diversion to false idols. (J.L.H. 'Resurrection' within this category? — 1 Cor. 15 — i.e. here, the future in the light of Christ.) On the conduct of worship, and in particular the use of the fruits of the spirit, Paul's poor opinion of the practice of speaking with tongues is the arresting topic, surely, for twentieth century Christendom (1 Cor. 12-14). "I thank God that I speak in tongues more than you all; nevertheless, in church I would rather speak five words with my mind, in order to instruct others, than ten thousand words in a tongue." One of Paul's supreme saving graces is his blessed down-to-earth practicality. Another is his skill at reducing conundrums eventually to the love commandment.

It is this skill which is brought prominently into play when the apostle deals with the problems of daily living presented to him for solution by the Corinthians. The major problems of this sort are problems of sexual morality and meat-eating. Most sensibly, he castigates the man who by living with his step-mother openly flaunts the consanguinity laws not only of budding Christendom but of the pervading heathen society. This is going too far. (1 Cor. 5). But his view on other problems of sexual morality — marry rather than burn, seem to stem from the basic commonsense already mentioned, and in the case of the woman with rights over her husband's body as well as (naturally in that period) vice versa, he advises a mutuality of love well in advance of the times (1 Cor. 7). It is clear, however, that Paul's judgments in these matters are greatly influenced by eschatological considerations.

26

Concerning food offered to idols (1 Cor. 8), he weaves his way through a series of arguments to finish inexorably at the love commandment; "Only take care lest this liberty of yours somehow become a stumbling-block to the weak" (1 Cor. 8:9), and "If food is a cause of my brother's falling, I will never eat meat, lest I cause my brother to fall" (1 Cor. 8:13). Many a devoted husband or wife in our present times has forsworn alcohol or tobacco in this spirit.

If a footnote may be permitted, it concerns the impression made on the reader of the Corinthian Epistles of Paul wrestling with these problems. His boasts of weakness are no empty boasts: at times he does come over as weak or at any rate diffident (1 Cor. 2:3). (J.L.H. Felt *much* threatened by uncertainty over the apparent disloyalty at Corinth.) At others coldly furious (II Cor. 13. 3). Always he has to dig deep into his faith and also into his mind, to provide the instant answers; making up doctrine as he goes along. It is a pity that so much inspiration should have been fossilised by later generations.

22nd, 23rd, 24th January 1985

My dear E,

This is the long-contemplated reply to your letter of 9th December, but no thunderbolt, I fear. Thunderbolts are not part of my armoury at present. I enclose a copy of your letter, for by now you may have forgotten what you wrote.

Here we go: seriatim.

1) *'One studies theology, one experiences religion or doesn't'*

At first sight this would appear a very clear and logical distinction; but how many would-be Christians actually 'experience' religion, I ask myself. And how do they recognise it to be 'religious' experience? Is there any difference between this type of experience and the experience of singing Bach or Vivaldi? Or other experiences of looking and listening? Are they different in kind, as experiences? Even suppose you limit a religious experience to the operation of the Holy Spirit — how do you say with certainty that it is so? The other day I heard an extract on the radio from the biography of Pope John XXIII. He

thought the Holy Spirit had told him to hold the Vatican
Council, but Pope and all, he was none too sure and took all sorts
of steps to reassure himself that this was not his own pride
covertly persuading him on this course. Speaking personally, I
have seen sad letters from schizophrenic patients addressed
personally to one or other member of the Trinity, with whom
they believe themselves to be in direct and private
communication, so that I am jolly wary of this type of experience.
Yet Paul undoubtedly had it. And unless the emotions are
involved to provide a degree of motivation, inertia (acidie — the
mediaeval deadly sin?) sets in, in this as in every other field.
Speaking personally again (and introspection can be a valid
research tool) *I* find myself impelled to try to be a Christian not
because of experiences, but because contemplation of the
Christian ethos (or is that too remote? Should one out with it and
say gospel?) produces the most satisfying available explanation
of this life and its values — the best fit, as sociologists say. Isn't
that theology?

2)   *"I'm perfectly sure that you may not pick and choose among
testaments to suit yourself: The God of Christianity is the God of
the Old Testament, never doubt that. You accept or reject the
package".*

I couldn't disagree more, and this is the crux of the matter. If
you think like this, you miss the whole point of the coming of
Christ, and of Christianity, and in fact the New Testament itself.
"For if justification were through the law (i.e. Judaism resulting
from the Jewish perception of God as portrayed in the Old
Testament) — then Christ died to no purpose". (Gal. 2:21.) And
again, "For in Jesus Christ neither circumcision (i.e. the law) nor
uncircumcision (i.e. the life-style of the Gentiles) is of any avail,
but faith working through love." (Gal. 5:6.)

Of course the New Testament is riddled through and through
with Old Testament ideas and prophecies. It could not be
otherwise. If you have a historical Christ, an actual man, he had
to be born into an actual historical setting, and this was it. But
the point is that he not only fulfilled the Old Testament, he
transformed it. (To say he re-interpreted it is also true, but the
word is too shadowy to use here.) If Christ had simply fulfilled

Old Testament Jewish aspirations, and had been the type of Messiah they were looking for, they need never have bothered to have him put to death.

3)   *Doesn't it strike you as perhaps the least little bit patronising to say that Paul was as it were tainted with O.T. habits of thought? He was an Old Testament Jew, surely, through and through.*

The answer is No: I don't think it patronising and not for one moment am I suggesting that he was "tainted" with O.T. habits of thought. I agree with you, he was an Old Testament Jew through and through, and in fact is often obliged to recite his credentials as a Jew when he is preaching to the Jews. But the whole point about Paul is that he was so much *more* than the Old Testament Jew he started out as — Pharisee of the Pharisees, holding the cloaks of the stoners of Stephen and so forth. After his vision on the road to Damascus, he was convinced that he was called to preach to the Gentiles and this landed him in an entirely new ballgame, if one may put it like that. Hence the extraordinary complications he got into in Romans, struggling to work out for himself what preaching to the Gentiles entailed, the whole process rendered more difficult, as I see it, because his mental processes could not help being those of a born Pharisee, while all the time he was struggling to breach the new ground of non-Jewry. It strikes me that at times he found the whole reconciling process too much of a good job — reconciling Jew and Gentile, that is. Witness the famous "all things to all men" passage in I Corinthians (9: 19-23).

Back to your letter. I think we have dealt with the Jewishness of Christ earlier, except for the crucial 'redemption from sin by his blood' which is the explicit statement both of Jewish sacrificial victim and Christian truth.

4)   *"What you call (and I don't dissent) the archaic primitive ideas of the blood of sin offering are surely not only specifically Christian but Jesus's own ideas in his own language, from his own tradition and teaching? Redemption from sin by his blood was after all his idea (synoptic gospels: can't find it in John). I thought it was the sacred heart of the creed? I'm sorry to have to reiterate that I find it wholly repugnant and rather mad."*

29

This is all part of the same theme, albeit the central, and if you like, most sacred part of the theme. To recap: Christ was a Jew and all the disciples were Jews, and, obtuse lot as they were, he had to get his message through to them in terms that they (and he) understood. Hence (as I see it, and I may be even heretically free thinking here — I simply don't know), the confusing O.T. format and clothing of the N.T. message. As I see it, it took Paul — soaked and permeated with the crucifixion and resurrection, to bring out the crucial (lit) novelty of the Christian gospel. to detach it from its O.T. roots. After the fall of Jerusalem, I understood, and the spread of the gospel among the Gentiles, the early Church had other more pressing problems to contend with, like heretics and persecutions. In the first post-crucifixion decades, as during the early life of Jesus, the main problem was the relationship with Judaism.

Of course all this leaves many problems unsolved. It always will. One of the main puzzles seems to me to centre round the consciousness of Jesus. If at one moment he was confined within the thought processes of Judaism and guilt-offerings, at others he was making these stupendous claims of identity and sonship with God himself. No wonder we get mixed up. In the latter capacity the demonstration of the power of absolute love is used to transcend the O.T. metaphors.

If all this by-passes doctrines of redemption, and guilt, and a jealous God, I'm sorry but we haven't done that yet! On a superficial level, I can't in any event reconcile a jealous God with a God of love.

You wrote 'Quo vadis'. I reply "I don't know, but it's very exciting."

Love Nancy

25th January 1985

Dear Nancy,

Thanks for the splendid Epistle. You and Paul! I reply, equally *seriatim*;

1.   How can one be a Christian without experiencing religion?

30

Of course it's different from experiencing music. It's because Paul 'had it' that I dislike and distrust Paul. No, the idea of being Christian because that provides the most satisfying available explanation of life and its values is not theology. More like autobiography.

2.   I say: The God of Christianity is Jehovah. You say: to think like this is to miss the whole point of Christ and Christianity and in fact the N.T. itself. I reply: to think otherwise is to *invent* the whole point. I mean, suppose there *isn't* (as for me and the billionfold majority of the species past present and future) a point? What if Christ (Gal. 2.21) *did* die to no purpose?

You're not allowed (by my rules!) to write down the answer to the sum beforehand and then point to those selected factors which, multiplied together, produce it. What's the *evidence* that it's the *right* answer?

If you begin also by saying that it's the right answer because it's the right answer for you (as per (1) above) then why can't I say that it's therefore the wrong answer because it's the wrong answer for me?

If the New Testament is riddled (the *mot juste!*) with the Old Testament, and could not be otherwise, can it *really* be all that amazingly different?

The argument about the Jews not needing to put Jesus to death looks rather two edged to me. As that diabolical atheist Christopher Marlowe was accused of saying: if the Jews crucified Jesus, it was they that knew him best.

Besides, they *didn't*: that ancient scandal, furthermore, fuelled the furnaces of Dachau. It was surely the *Romans* who put him to death? Crucifixion was never a *Jewish* form of capital punishment, was it?

3.   I don't see what, exactly, makes Paul (or Jesus, come to that) anything other than Jews preaching a Jewish religion. The fact that it was preached *to the Gentiles* is surely a confirmation, not a disproof, of that basic and obvious fact? Of course one may explain that they chose to speak in those terms because only in those terms could they be understood; but what's wrong with the

simpler explanation that they said what they said because that's what they actually *meant*?

4.   All that *stuff* about blood and pain and sacrifice, as I see it (namely with distress and distaste) is absolutely *not* novel, not in any way nor by one hair's breadth detached from the O.T. roots. It is the very language of sacrificial ritual, or witch-doctor mumbo-jumbo. What exactly is supposed to be different about it? God is to Jesus as Abraham to Isaac, i.e. murderous, in an allegedly benevolent sort of way.

You say that Jesus was sometimes (how often?) confined within the thought-processes of Judaism and guilt offerings etc., but at other times made claims of identity (where?) and sonship with God. But surely if the first part of that is right, then the claims must *also* be within those same thought processes? How could they not have been, except by conjuring or cheating? And it further seems to me that such claims were always part of Jewish O.T. monotheism. Moses already was on terms of easy and affable intimacy with God. It was only after detailed personal discussion that he was able to reduce the commandments to *only ten*, I bet.

13th March 1985

My dear E,

I enclose another essay, not yet written, which will be the very reverse of triumphant since neither the subject nor this type of minute scholarship turn one on at all. I suppose this is because it is more than usually second-hand. When writing about Paul one felt (probably quite erroneously) that one could somehow get inside the skin of the man through the maze of translation, interpretation and conjecture. Not so with the gospels so far. (J.L.H. Oh! I'm sorry.)

A further apologia. The essay is required to deal only with the first two chapters of Luke's gospel and in my innocence I thought ` this could not be other than self-limiting and straightforward; and would absolve one from the compulsion that arises to speculate and philosophize on the slenderest basis of knowledge conceivable: (worse than the commentators because so

32

ignorant). How wrong can one be.

I can remember writing to you earlier that dishing up lecture notes was not my idea of essay-writing. Well I'm reduced to that. Though one could I suppose do worse because they are so *good* when seen against the other commentators and thus judged on their own level. It's just I suppose that my hard-learnt researcher's habits stick around and one becomes innoculated against accepting other types of learning on the nod, as it were (since we don't know Greek or Hebrew nor, I suspect, do we understand the ramifications of that ever-useful concept *midrash*, of which I am becoming increasingly suspicious).

All love, Nancy

What Luke intended to convey in the Birth Stories in Chapters I and II.

'Luke begins, not with the cross, not with the baptism of Jesus, not even with his birth nor with the birth of his immediate predecessor John the Baptist, but with the promise to the Baptist's father. The setting at the centre of Jewry, with the entire nation present, together with the hitherto unprecedented reach backwards in time, are symptomatic of the conscious bid for historical continuity which marked Luke's generation of Christians.' (Drury, p. 46.)

This is the crux of the matter. Luke's peculiar beginning (which results, incidentally in the genealogy of Jesus being pushed back to the end of Chapter 3), must be regarded primarily as evidence of its author's view of history and the place of Jesus in it. When Luke/Acts are regarded as the two-volume* masterpiece established by modern criticism, the author's objective becomes clear. Backwards in time stretch the scriptures, with their wealth of prophecy to be fulfilled. At centre stage (but low in terms of christological study) comes Jesus, embodiment of prophetic fulfilment but yielding too to charismatic, existential primacy. Then later, in Acts, his own

---

* "The former treatise O Theophilus" becomes prosaically "Vol One, to Theophilus", as one commentator remarks.

prophecies are fulfilled in the coming of the spirit and the preaching of the gospel to the ends of the earth. The whole concept portrays a historical sweep which is simply not present in the other gospels.

How does it all work out in practice in the opening two chapters of Luke's gospel?

As a start, the very style is seen as significant, the style of the septuagint or old Greek testament rather than the *Koine* or common Greek employed elsewhere. John Drury, surely one of the most effective of Lucan specialists, carries out the necessarily minute analysis which establishes this beyond doubt, listing in an appendix the septuagintal phrases also to be found in Luke 1 and 2. Thus, for example, Luke 1:28, the angels' greeting "The Lord is with you" occurs frequently in the LXX, and specifically at Judges 6:12. Many other parallels are cited. The effect, according to Leslie Houlden, is not only to convey the meaning conveyed by identical words, but to accentuate the scriptural validity of the new narrative, to authorise Jesus in the eyes of Jewry.

A similar and even more striking effect is obtained when whole passages are quoted. The classic example here is the *Magnificat* (Luke 1:46) Mary's poem of praise found on inspection so closely to resemble Hannah's song (I Samuel 2) which she sang after the birth of Samuel. Again, the prophecy of John the Baptist's father Zechariah, familiar in the liturgy as the *Benedictus*, and Simeon's song the *Nunc Dimittis*, are redolent of Old Testament sentiment and phraseology, and faithfully referenced back, in the case of Simeon, to Isaiah.

'To turn from Luke to Old Testament narrative . . . is to cross no boundaries but to remain in the same country, to hear the same language in the same forms describing similar events. Why? The answer is simple and takes us deeper still: because the same God who as Lord of history works his purpose out by prophecy and fulfilment as year succeeds to year, is working all in all.

There is no interruption because Luke is joined to Judaism at the deepest and most unbreakable point: historical monotheism. What Haenchen has said of Acts is true of the

34

gospel. In reality it is God himself — the supreme authority — who governs and prescribes, in accordance with his plan, the course to be followd by the "Word of God".' (Drury 7.)

Luke's attitude to Judaism, institution as well as literature is further instanced by his treatment of the temple in the birth narrative. It is at the temple, at the very moment when it is his turn to burn the sacred incense, that Zechariah is accosted by the angel with the good news of his impending fatherhood, "with the whole multitude of the people praying outside". It is at the temple that old Simeon takes up the child Jesus into his arms; and Anna the prophetess, fasting and praying there "coming up at that very hour she gave thanks to God and spoke of him to all who were looking for the redemption of Jerusalem" (2:36).

If these prophetic forerunners were rooted in the ark of the covenant, Jesus too, in the Lucan narrative, remained fast within the tradition during his boyhood — albeit already pointing beyond. In the Passover story, when he was twelve years old, it was in the temple that his anxious parents found him, sitting among the teachers, listening and asking questions, fitting easily into the temple scene.

The above represents part of the accepted wisdom (all there is time for, SNW). From it consequences flow. About it, questions must be asked. The first consequence is of the rather esoteric, specialist kind, namely, that Q, that elusive, speculative written source, may be dispensed with, as already demanded by the application of Occam's razor. For if the Septuagint can so demonstrably and unequivocally provide the source for all Lucan material outside Mark and Matthew, what need is there for Q?

But does the Septuagint satisfactorily provide all sources? Yes, by postulating that Luke made wide use of the *midrash* technique says (so far as I can make out), one school, among whom John Drury and Don Cupitt (and J.L.H.?) may be counted. Perhaps — but not entirely satisfactorily because of the unsatisfactory nature of *midrash* when viewed with any degree of historical criticism; this would be the alternative view. Did the Gospel events take place or didn't they? What is there to stop them all being nothing but *midrash*? (Drury, page 44 refers.)

It is almost an anticlimax to mention, in the wake of such a seemingly mighty problem, a further doubt which obtrudes when considering the methodology of attribution of intent. Once again, Drury too has picked up a doubt which has been simmering in this student's mind for many weeks. "How can the reader be sure that the meaning the critic sees is the meaning the writer intended? . . . how can he be sure that the critic's flight of imagination follows the author's? A mind as ingeniously poetic as Austin Farrer's could well be taking off on its own." (J.L.H. No, the reader can't be sure: the experts differ in quality and view — but there *is* a certain progress in the subject, e.g. Drury is in some ways more aware of Jewish models than Farrer was — and such improved historical scholarship can only be an advantage). (p 42.) And Drury demands some kind of historical check. His own solution is the use of *midrash*. Is this historically satisfactory?

15th March 1985

My dear Nancy,

Luke leaves me cold. Thus what you call portraying a historical sweep (with a broad brush?) and what Houlden calls accentuating the scriptual validity of the narrative are what I call plain fraudulance. I mean, Luke must have known perfectly well that (for example) the words he attributes to Mary are just his own invention or rather plagiarism from Samuel. Gives an entirely new slant on the Bethlehem crib. Admittedly *Ave Hannah* doesn't sound so good. But what foxes me is — why does anyone bother with people who perpetuate such practices? Why study the gospel according to St. Fake?

Of course someone like Drury would find this a pretty profound phenomenon, linking the O. and N.T., so that the two can be exactly the same as well as (in a mystery) utterly different, as the preconceived beliefs require.

And what, if not Hebrew for eyewash, is *midrash*? [12] It sounds like a symptom of prickly heat. Isn't it what less learned or committed people call forgery? But perhaps this is what you're (very daringly) asking. Is it all nothing but mad trash? Well, I suppose it must be a bit better than that, or at least more

36

seemingly reputable: but to me its mapped coastline looks amazingly congruent with the wilder shores of Shakespeare scholarship. And after all if people couldn't persuade themselves of *absolutely anything* no matter how unevidenced or implausible there wouldn't ever have been any Christian or other religion in the first place. I seem to recall, as a small boy, seeing a banner headline in the *News of the World* that ran: WAS IT THE VIRGIN MARY THAT MRS. O'REILLY SAW FROM THE SCULLERY WINDOW? and thinking to myself that the answer was very probably 'no'.

With love as ever,
E

The course finished in March. I had half thought of taking, in May, the examination which forms part of the London University Extra-Mural Diploma in Religious Studies. But I soon changed my mind after a glance at a previous year's paper: this was not something that could be knocked off at will, but would require old-fashioned hard work and this I could not commit myself to in view of the illness situation in the family. However, I had written four essays of a sort and was boiling up for another. One couldn't do a six-month course on the New Testament, complete with essay-writing without attempting something on the Fourth Gospel, I thought. Leslie Houlden very kindly agreed to look at it though it was after term and the hunt for marks and units was no longer on.

Easter 1985.

How did the Fourth Gospel present the person of Christ?

Present day Biblical scholars assert that it is wrong to regard the Fourth Gospel as more theological than the synoptics: the writers of the latter also possess their own theological standpoints and should not be viewed as mere compilers or anthologists, gleaners of other men's seed-corn. The scholars must have a point, but could they also be stating a tautology? For surely any act of composition or of compilation involves writing from a standpoint, exercising choice and employing categories. Whether one needs to call this theology seems a moot

37

point. (J.L.H. It's theology if it's a standpoint involving ideas about God.) What is on the other hand clear is that the Fourth Gospel is much more overtly metaphysical than the other three; in it 'narrative is the servant of conceptual theology, not its master' (*Patterns of Faith*, J.L.H. p.44). Thus it presents the deepest quarry for philosophical mining of the four, and anyone daring to dig there must in turn be strictly selective if he is ever going to finish!

In the first half of the essay, therefore, will be presented ideas on the person of Christ as God, and in the second half the person of Christ as man, in each case drawing on gospel narrative peculiar to John. The coda will hint at the implications. (And even as one writes the words, one recoils at the sheer effrontery of it.) To make a start: It is *only* in John that Jesus is presented as *preaching himself*, and in fact, in the last resort, as equating himself with God. (J.L.H. Not quite — but this aspect dominates John.) This occurs in the 'I am' declarations *tout court* (also 20.28 etc.), over which so much agonizing has taken place. Their symbolic elaborations, with a predicate after the verb, occasion less difficulty.

Two passages stand out when considering these declarations of identity with God (*pace* C.K. Barrett and given that we are not attempting to describe the mode of this identity). The first is at 8:58: "Truly, truly, I say to you, before Abraham was, I am". (R.S.V.) In his discussion of these matters, Barrett mysteriously dismisses this saying as "soon fall(ing) out of the discussion for the main sense here is that of the continuous being of the Son — he exists before Abraham, now and for ever". (*Essays on John*, p. 12.) Well, good grief. If this is not a problem, what is? (J.L.H. I suppose C.K.B. is thinking *within* the flow of John's narrative.)

The second passage in this context comes at 18: 4, 5, 6.

"Then Jesus . . . said to them 'Whom do you seek?' They answered him 'Jesus of Nazareth.' Jesus said to them 'I am (he).' Judas, who betrayed him, was standing with them. When he said to them 'I am (he)', they drew back and fell to the ground." (R.S.V.)

The last five words give the clue. The words translated

variously as 'I am he', or 'I am', or 'I am the one who', or 'I am who I am', as in Exodus 3:14, denoted the Jewish Jahveh, the name for God which was too holy to pronounce, and which, when the Jews there present heard pronounced, caused them to fall to the ground in awe. Barrett, in his effort to explain all this away, is despite his great learning less than convincing.

These are the prime unequivocal claims purported to be spoken by Jesus himself, the raw stuff of creeds and the stated beliefs of later centuries — 'of one substance with the Father'. Not spoken by Jesus, but by the writer(s) of the Fourth Gospel, is the identification of him with the word of God, the Logos, the symbol of God's creative activity and also for the expression of his revelation. Whence the symbolism derives, whether from the Platonism of the Hellenists or, as later scholarship now renders more likely, from the Wisdom literature of the Old Testament, is in a sense immaterial. The point is that the Word is uttered, in Christ, through Christ. It is God's will thus to reveal himself, because this is his nature. (See Painter, p. 27.)

Propositions of this sort raise immense problems relating to the pre-existence of Christ, to the self-consciousness of Christ, and to Trinitarian doctrine in general. It is impossible to discuss them here (but see J.L.H.'s 'Doctrine of the Trinity and the Person of Christ', p. 25 in *Explorations in Theology*), and impossible to resolve them ever. They are not those sort of questions. Unfathomable mystery (to use J.L.H.'s words) they may be. To the present writer, with the haziest memories of a special paper on the *Critique of Pure Reason*, they appear as questions outside space and time with which finite minds are simply not equipped to deal. Same thing. (J.L.H. One might still see how such ideas arose for the writer: from a conviction that Jesus filled every niche of mediation between God and man — and this for him included 'wisdom' ideas, derived from *his* kind of training in Judaism.)

The Fourth Gospel in fact teems with further instances of Christ's self-revelation, perhaps marginally more possible to comprehend since the symbolism of the teaching is illustrative rather than absolute, and the appearances too are individual in character, to selected (self-selected?) people. A few examples follow.

Considering first the pre-resurrection revelations of his earthly life, these are to the woman of Samaria at the well: "I know the Messiah is coming, he who is called Christ . . . I who speak to you am he." (4: 24, 25); to the blind beggar: "And who is he, Sir, that I may believe? . . . You have seen him, and it is he who speaks to you" (9: 36, 37) (of whom more later). They are followed by the post-resurrection appearances: to Mary Magdalene when she took him for the gardener (20: 17), and above all, the experience with Thomas the doubting disciple, with his final capitulation "My Lord and my God" (20: 28). In each case, individual recognition suddenly dawns: recognition of his physical presence or manifestation.

The Gospel is of course also profoundly rich in teaching by symbolism. Jesus knew what he was about (if one may comment thus without irreverence) when he chose to impart his teaching through these more substantial vehicles.

Painter makes the point that all the symbolism in John is christologically orientated (whereas this is not so of the parables). Thus Christ is identified with the Bread of Life (6: 35, 41, 48); as the light of the world (8; 12, 9: 5); the door (10: 7, 9); the good shepherd (10: 11, 14); the resurrection and the life (11: 25); the way, the truth and the life (14: 6) and the true vine (15: 1, 5). Each presents a powerful aspect of self-revelation, originally no doubt in contradistinction to Israel and Jewry, subsequently found to be universally relevant: Though the exclusivity of the Way, the Truth and the Life saying raises particular difficulty in a twentieth century ethnically conscious Britain unsure how Christianity ought to relate to other faiths.

More direct (and therefore less easily comprehended) teaching supplements the symbolism in many passages, in which Christ proclaims himself as in the Father, and the Father in him (14: 10) hammering home to his disciples the essence of their future belief.

The second half of this essay attempts to consider how the writer of the Fourth Gospel presents the person of Christ in his human aspect. All the passages, which are peculiar to the Fourth Gospel, illustrate the meaning of love, and from a very cursory glance at some of the literature recommended, this

40

would seem to constitute an original approach to the subject.

Explicitly, the new commandment is given at Chapter 13, verse 34.

> "A new commandment I give to you, that you love one another; even as I have loved you, that you also love one another. By this all men will know that you are my disciples, if you have love one for another" (R.S.V.)

It is repeated and expanded upon in the succeeding discourses (incidentally lending support to the textual critical view that so much repetition must denote the work of many hands). One further instance (at 15: 12) must suffice.

> "This is my commandment, that you love one another as I have loved you. Greater love has no man than this, that a man lay down his life for his friends. You are my friends if you do what I command you" (R.S.V.)

Three passages will be quoted considering Jesus as love in action.

At first sight the healing of the blind man, so graphically related in Chapter 9, and so revealingly illustrating the staunchness of the man — his exasperation at constantly repeating his story — his fearless repartee — may be thought to demonstrate Jesus' capacity to heal rather than his capacity to love. (Or are they the same?) But we come to the end of the story, when the Jews excommunicated the man from the synagogue (9: 35). Not content with healing him, Jesus takes the trouble to go back when he hears of this, finds him, and so to speak, finishes the job.

The Lazarus story depicts, among many other things, another aspect of human love in action, its vulnerability. The Fourth Gospel makes it abundantly clear that Jesus was deeply fond of Lazarus and his family:

> "When Jesus saw her weeping, and the Jews who came with her also weeping he was deeply moved in spirit and troubled and he said: 'Where have you laid him?'"

> "They said to him 'Lord, come and see.' Jesus wept. So the

Jews said 'See how he loved him.'" (11: 33-36).

It is in this Gospel pre-eminently that this tender, vulnerable aspect of Christ personified as love may be perceived. The last demonstration of the meaning of love in action is furnished by the washing of the disciples' feet. After Peter's typical emotional outburst and misunderstanding "You shall never wash my feet", Jesus points up the final emphasis on service.

"If I then, your Lord and Teacher, have washed your feet, you also ought to wash one another's feet" (13: 1-20)

(J.L.H. I think he sees the "divine one" as the marvellous expresser of these 'human' traits: — and *that's* the wonder.)

Coda

No wonder the Fourth Gospel occupies the place it does in christological doctrine on the one hand and the affections of the faithful on the other. Christ is God: Christ is love, and this is another reason for the affirmation that God is love, the first being, of course, that God so loved the world that he sent his only begotton Son: the whole doctrine of the Incarnation.

It has still not really sunk in. So powerful remains O.T. influence, so pervasive was the need felt even by Jesus himself to fulfil O.T. prophesies, that God the Father is still often conceived of in O.T. terms, omnipotent, ruler of heaven and earth, provoking "thy wrath and indignation against us". But if Christ is God, then God too is vulnerable. John Taylor, until recently Bishop of Winchester, is believed to be about to write a book on the suffering God. Is not this idea likely to get nearer to the heart of the matter than the O.T. hangover of, say, propitiation for sin, an idea singularly absent from the thought of the Fourth Gospel?

(J.L.H. This came together well, didn't it?)

Later

Dear E,

I've been looking at my notes and find I can comment on several of your points which escaped in the rush. Contemplating the nature of the original manuscripts, you wrote (on October 16th 1984):

What were the scriptures written on, in and with, I wonder?

Well, until printing was invented in the fifteenth century, all the writing was done by hand on at first papyrus then parchment sheets. The early Christians were the first to develop a book-like format, which they employed for the first copies of the New Testament. The earliest extant fragments, dating from the second century are in codex form and not scroll form.

You also wrote in the same letter about the prevalence of Greek and about whether Jesus spoke any as well as the presumed Aramaic. My notes say that he probably did. *A propos* of which, I turned on the car radio the other day and found myself in the middle of a programme pointing to geographical enclaves in Syria and Turkey where Aramaic, now mysteriously become Syriac, still persists. I was too late to catch what was said about the precise link between A and S, which is a pity.

Back to Greek. It was very widespread and used even in Jerusalem, in the very heart of Judaism, where rulers of the synagogue — as it were church-wardens — built synagogues complete with baths. Jewish funeral urns or ossuaries containing bones have been found carrying Greek inscriptions. Often people had both Hebrew and Greek names, e.g.; Saul: Paul Cephas: Peter. Probably these two possessed their two names all along. It wasn't that they were re-christened later, so to speak.

Isn't it fascinating about the ossuaries?

Coming to a later letter, you wrote on March 15, 1985 on the subject of Luke, whose Gospel seems not to be the favourite of either of us:

> "I mean, Luke must have known perfectly well that (for example) the words he attributes to Mary are just his own invention or rather plagiarism from Samuel. Gives an entirely new slant to the Bethlehem crib. Admittedly, *Ave Hannah* doesn't sound so good . . . Why study the Gospel according to St. Fake?"

Well, of course it isn't a question of faking, but of the literary conventions of the period. Originality and personal authenticity quite simply were not prized. Things weren't like that: the great thing was to show that one belonged to the tradition. To do this, it was considered quite O.K., for instance, to borrow, and write under the name of, some revered figure, which is why some of the Epistles are so difficult to attribute, I gather.

Another form it took was the case in point, quoting wholesale from the scriptures (O.T. to us). Another example of this I am rather sad about. That lovely passage in Philippians 2: 6-11 "Have this mind among yourselves, which is yours in Christ Jesus" etc. is widely thought to be not original Paul at all, but a quote from a pre-existing hymn or form of worship. If you look up the *Good News* translation, you find the passage set out in blank verse. I was so astonished, indeed upset, that I asked a question in class, which was quite bold of me, as there is very little time for questions. I asked what type of evidence was used to make this supposition. Leslie Houlden in reply described the U-form shape of that part of the manuscript.

It is all part and parcel of critical historical method, getting to comprehend the conventions and the intellectual climates in which the different authors lived. And because it is so utterly alien to our own intensely individualistic concepts of authorship, and indeed to our very thought processes, it takes a lot of doing, a lot of conscious effort. That's what I find, anyhow.

NOTES

YEAR I

Except for Leslie Houlden's note on *midrash*, these are essay references, the rest of J.L.H.'s tutor's comments being retained in the text.

1. p. 5   *Historical Introduction to the New Testament.* Grant. 1963. Introduction — p. 25.
2. p. 6   *How to read the New Testament.* Etienne Charpentier. 1981. p. 8.
3. p. 7   Charpentier. p. 120.
4. p. 9   Grant. p. 35.
5. p. 9   Grant. p. 35.
6. p. 12   *Wrestling with Romans* by John Robinson, S.C.M. Press.
7. p. 12   *The New Testament Letters* by J.W.C. Wand. O.U.P. 1946. *Letters to Young Churches* by J.B. Phillips. Bles. 1946.
8. p. 14   *Pauline Pieces* by Morna Hooker. Epworth Press. 1979.
9. p. 16   Ibid. p. 42.

10. p. 17 Other aspects of Paul's doctrine, such as the concept of the righteousness of God, have had to be omitted for sheer lack of time. Also the meanings of the word 'flesh'.
11. p. 17 See Romans 12.
12. p. 36 J.L.H.

There has been a tendency to use the term *midrash* too loosely: it was in fact a controlled set of techniques for 'seeing' meaning in the text of the Jewish law, eithet in the O.T. Books of Moses, or, by 200 A.D., in the Mishnah which wrote down the oral law (also believed by them to go back — by oral tradition — to Moses).

It is technically an error to use *midrash* of looser romances etc. in Jewish writing based on O.T. stories but moving on from those models: it is probable that Luke uses O.T. stories in the way Jewish romances do, but it is an error, I think, to use the *term midrash* to describe the process.

SECOND YEAR

My dear E,

Time to get back to work after a long summer lay-off — perhaps too long. I'm finding it hard to get my mind round the subjects under discussion, and equally hard to sit myself down for a consecutive three-hour spell. Peggy quite briskly told me the other day that my various good works(!) — comforting the sick and bereaved and so forth — amounted to an excuse for not getting on. If I was working full-time there would *have* to be time for everything. She of course is permanently in double over-drive — fifth gear as we now call it, which means that at the highest speeds one kind of coasts on less fuel. Rather apt for her.

It also seems time to re-cap. When I was at Ampleforth Jo asked which bits of the New Testament we covered last year. I had (again) quite a difficulty in remembering (because you can't do the lot). Isn't that shaming too? But since one of my objectives in the whole enterprise is to find out what is being taught in the theological colleges (which for this purpose includes the Southwark Ordination Course, which uses our Centre), I had better re-cap on our syllabus. The first three lectures gave general background: how the N.T. came into existence, methods of study and criticism, and the cultural setting of Judaism and the Gentile world. Then we had four lectures on Paul, his writings, career, teaching, theology concentrating on Romans, Galatians and Corinthians. Two lectures each on Mark, Matthew, Luke — Acts: three on the Johannine community and its writings and three on "What did Jesus do and teach? Who was he?" A lecture on the Passion and Resurrection narratives, one on Hebrews, and the last, rather a hotch-potch to finish up with, on Ephesians and the Pastoral Epistles and Paul's successors. Nothing on Revelation and very little on Acts by itself.

I think it's also worth commenting on lecture method. Leslie

Houlden went in for the old-fashioned talking, exposition, lecture and short discussion (sadly short for one nurtured on tutorials — but time presses so in these extra-mural, evening settings). And we all sat round and took notes, or in some cases, taped it. I think the very act of note-taking aides assimilation and understanding, keeps one alert to précis where possible and generally helps.

Our present tutor, Alan Race, lecturing on doctrine, uses what is presumably a more modern method, with visual aids such as sheafs of notes which are passed round, and which he then talks to, on, about. This method certainly ensures that the student goes away with *something* — viz., reams of typed material. But I find I don't digest it the same way and wonder if I am unique in this? I also wonder whether this method, which I presume to be rampant in our schools, may contribute to general illiteracy, for note-taking is a painless, private way of practising written articulation.

I know that you favour the acquisition of knowledge strictly via books and seldom went to any lectures as an undergraduate. Me too; just some in my first year and increasingly few thereafter. But then our situation was different. Theoretically we had all the time in the world to research and write our essays. Extra-mural students mostly do a full day's work and *then* start: I do have the greatest admiration for them.

I've also been looking through our last year's correspondence and your comments on it. There is a good deal of unfinished business which I will deal with as soon as I can; indeed I thought I had already, some of it, but you appear not to have taken a blind bit of notice!

The main points, I think, are. Do you agree?

1. The nature of theology.

2. Your letter of November 23 in which you abhor the language of God being 'satisifed' with the crucifixion.

3. Your letter of December 9 "I'm perfectly sure you cannot pick and choose among testaments to suit yourself. You accept or reject the package". I've got a lot to say about that, still. It's coming soon.

4.   On a quite different level, you write that I should address
     myself to your *difficulties*. But what is an atheist or
     humanist doing admitting difficulties? Your stance is clear.
     There is no God. What is the nature of your difficulties? Are
     you saying you wish you could be a Christian if only it
     weren't for the lack of hard proof and intellectual
     respectability?

In general, I don't think you are as way out as you suppose.
And since I'm a bit way on, the chances are that we shall
eventually converge. We may converge on the following
propositions: that God is the *summmum bonum*: and that the
summmum bonum must be God, some broad statement of this
kind which can mean everything or nothing. All the bits
you object to as distasteful must be something other than
God-given i.e. they must spring from man at a certain epoch
in history and be therefore relative, partial and always
changing.

Turning to my original objectives in the light of the first
year, I have decided to omit altogether discussion of the work
ethic. It is too far removed, both in time and theme, from the
origins of Christianity — work and works being two entirely
different concepts. On the other hand, the subject of the relationship of Christianity to other faiths is turning out to be
very *à propos*. And if the Polkinghorne can be traced, I would
love a potted résumé of the present science/religion position
from a top-rank physicist. Splitting the atom has certainly
melted this too too solid flesh and introduced a quite new
scenario.

Back to the present. As last year, our class numbers about
25, pretty equally split among the sexes. Only one from last
year, a very bright young-looking middle-aged woman who,
since last year, has been accepted as being suitable to train
as a deaconess. Alan Race our tutor is a young man who was
until recently an Anglican Chaplain of Kent University at
Canterbury — an ex-pupil of Leslie Houlden, I understand.
During the summer I read his good short book summarising
the different Christian positions adopted in relation to
other faiths; a subject of pressing practical as well as

theoretical importance in multi-racial Britain. Several students I find — at coffee and in general chat — are testing the water to see whether to become ordained: a nice bearded young teacher sitting next to me is one.

All love Nancy

October 1985

Dear Nancy,

Thanks for your lovely lively long letter.

You underestimate, however, the force and passion of my opposition to Christianity as ancient Jewish occultism crazed with blood and torture and sin. One of these loonies called here the other day to explain that they were having a week of Church Unity, which consisted of dishonestly pretending that all their daft squabbling denominations 'really' agreed, and that the rest of us who didn't (i.e. the 99% majority of the world's population) could expect at least a longish spell in outer darkness after our bodily death, while the Baptists (for these, no less, were the *illuminati* in question) laughed and exulted in the light and love of the living Lord. I implored these extraordinary people to pray for tolerance and humility: but I fear that my prayers will be unanswered.

They left me, conversely, unpersuaded. I fear that God as *Summun Bunkum* has much the same effect. Summum bonum surely means a human concept: virtue, knowledge, happiness or the like? Where were they to be found in history before humanity existed? Who was the God of the dinosaurs? (I know: Tyrannosaurus Rex Tremendae Majestatis.) Where are they to be found outside this planet now? Who is the extra-terrestrial God? (I know: the Flying Sorcerer.) Where in the world or out of it is the actual evidence for any good, summum or other, that is *not* human? or that *is* divine? And don't we also by the same argument need Satan and Summum Malum, or are we to blame humanity for all of that? I'm reminded of the various senses of the word

50

malo, thus:

> Malo, I would rather be,
> Malo, in adversity,
> Malo, than a naughty boy
> Malo, in an apple-tree.

How much more interesting language is than religion. Easier too.

I may not be your most typical reader; but I'm quite interested in history and chronology, and what I want to know is: what are the earliest references to Christianity (Tacitus? Suetonius?): what is the *evidence* for the dating of the Gospels and Pauline Epistles?

I'm mildly exasperated by Karen Armstrong's *The First Christian* (Pan. Channel 4) because it gives a table of significant events (good) and says lamely that some of the given dates will be a matter of controversy (i.e. we don't really know the significance of the significant events). But how can the way of the cross just ignore what's crucial?

Love E.

19 October 1985

Dear Nancy,

All very interesting and lively. Just two points about my comments as quoted. You can't choose among testaments, you accept the *package* (at least that's what I meant to say, not 'passage'!). Today's *Times* offers an instant illustration — both Elijah and Elisha obliged with an occasional raising from the dead, just like Jesus. It was presumably an old Jewish custom, though they do seem rather to have lost the knack of it since. Just think how useful it would have been in the Six Day War, for example. That brings me, with a rather deft turn, to the next point, namely the complaint that you don't address yourself to my difficulties. What I mean by 'my' difficulties are *those I'm pointing out*; for example that the raising of the dead by Elijah and Elisha are obviously just typical Jewish fiction and myth, or whatever is the latest polite name for lies and nonsense. The

51

atheist's main difficulty is the utter fantasy of postulating something or other doing something or other to the universe (matter, energy, space, time) from somewhere or other outside it: moving it about, meddling with it, loving it, sending a son into it, having said son tortured and killed in it, getting him back again as good as new, and so forth. Those are *a small selection* from among the *zillion* difficulties generated by this zany hypothesis. The main difficulty is that anyone in their senses should believe a word of it, not even (least of all) the word there allegedly was in the beginning.

Love as ever, E.

25 October 1985

Dear Nancy,

Lovely to see you: and I'm looking forward to the further contributions. Here's a further note on your four main points.

1. The nature of theology

2. God as Jehovah

3. Jehovah as Jesus's father

4. The difficulties

I define 4 as 1-3. Theology as I understand it (or, rather as I do *not* understand it) is the attempt to make sense about God: or, as I would tendentiously put it, the attempt to disguise nonsense as sense. I note that theology is an almost entirely *Christian* preoccupation or indeed obsession, and I attribute this to the fact that the Christian religion begins with, as absolute presuppositions, a set of bizarre assertions which take several lifetimes and billions of books to contort into any sort of rudimentary sense. One example among dozens is the belief in survival after death, in the face of the rather well known fact that nobody (but *nobody*) survives death, which is what death actually means.

Items 2-3 entail the special difficulty like Father like Son.

I should have thought that theology of all things would have to begin at the beginning, and that the first move that the writer of *Letters to an Atheist* has to make is to discharge the burden of proof that there is, or conceivably could be, any such being as the God of Christianity (e.g. an impersonal Person, a sexless Father, infinitely powerful yet possessing a will which his creatures ignore or reject *all the time*, infinitely good yet coexistent with evil, and so forth, in scores of such paradoxes). Of course theologians will *assume* this because it conveys a general licence to chatter to and about themselves and each other without bothering their heads about truth or sense or logic or argument or any such tiresome and inconvenient topics. But that's where and how you have to begin if you're writing to or for anyone outside the faith, surely?

Love as ever, E.

Sunday, November 3, 1985

Bentley

My dear E,

Many thanks for your October letters.

Here I am, staying with Bunch as so often these days, with an hour before lunch in which to let you know that I am *still* assembling the great ripostes and thought I might fill in with a running commentary on the Southwark lecture scene. We have had six lectures, quarter of the course, and I should have produced an essay. Not a hope. But I feel I should fill you in concerning the gist of things, foreign as I know it to be to the intellectual pattern of thinking which to you is the only way, and to me, far the most comfortable.

For the last two weeks we have been considering what present-day theologians, or some of them, call the theology of human nature.

For the first of these, we drew up a list of what are supposed to characterise the human condition, viz, rationality, morality, historicity, emotions, freedom, becoming and self-transcending, sexual differentiation, religious, emotions (affective sense).

What *can* this mean, I thought. Not even the parts of speech

53

are the same. I much prefer the older attempts at this exercise, for example Whale's,

> "Man is not a thinking, tool-using, laughing animal . . . but an animal made in the image of God which means that he is not an animal at all" . . .

So up I piped during questions, and asked Alan what discipline he was talking; that I found this all too vague to be meaningful; that people described human nature in terms of biology, medicine, psychology, sociology, anthropology, and these at least were disciplines one could understand and which meant *something*, though often with blurred edges.

I was told, charmingly, that I was a *reductionist* — a technical term which would be explained later, and that he was talking philosophy. Existentialism. But where does this get one? I must confess that I have never read Sartre or any of the others. But I begin to recognise the mode of thought: and that words used in this context, 'becoming', 'dynamism' etc. must mean something to somebody — even if not to me. And that I, as a reductionist, am accused of reducing the human condition to static categories, the sum of which taken together is insufficient fully to describe this condition. And that the something lacking is God.

The last clue in the puzzle was made clear the second week, when we got to the more familiar 'man created in the image of God' theme albeit in fresh phraseology. For instance, we were bidden to consider

> "Are there features in human experience which point to the God-relation at the heart of human nature?"

and to think of God

> "as summoning human beings to their full humanity through the choices and decisions they make".

So again I felt impelled to ask a question

> "Are you saying that we are commanded to become fully human rather than Christ-like?"

And there was quite a chorus which answered me, with Alan Race: "Same thing". I think I must choose an essay dealing with this mode of conceptualising. There must be *something* in it, she repeats doubtfully.

Walking back to Waterloo, I fell into step with a newcomer to the class. He too, was of riper years, a GP who retired three weeks ago and was approached by his Bishop with the suggestion that he should be ordained. "If you think that's a good idea", he replied, and here he is, ex-Cambridge, with this lifetime of doctoring and the easy manner of a sympathetic medic which is surely just the sort of person the Church can do with. He is being allowed to do the course in two years instead of three. We agreed that a good deal of what we hear is simply playing with words.

I must get this off — not that there's much to it.

Love Nancy

6 November 1985

Dear Nancy,

Many thanks for your Sunday letter. It makes me feel my age. I can now deal only in clear and distinct concepts such as the knight's move in chess, and can't manage even those (as the deletion demonstrates) all that well. Chess problems present problems; crossword puzzles puzzle me. All the rest is a faint thin piping heard from over the hill, and quite often round the bend as well. I can't read a 'thought' like Whale's "an animal made in the image of God and therefore not an animal at all" without reaching for my harpoon-gun. Who ever heard such degrading drivel? What are we to make of a concept x such that an entity has only to be x to be, also, what it is not, and further, simultaneously, not to be what it is, in a general nonconformist ecstasy of being and not being, as required? Or try analogues such as 'a jelly moulded in the shape of a teddy bear and *therefore not a jelly at all*' praise be. In a civilized and truly god-fearing society, anyone who used 'therefore' in such a (non)sense would be arrested and taken away in a plain van and on their way to the cells people would *throw stones* at them.

Love as ever, E.

55

Dear E,

Here is something on the first of our points at issue — viz., the nature of theology. See my letter of October 18th, yours of October 25th.

Nature of Theology

We were both pretty wide of the general mark when we exchanged views of the nature of theology months ago. But I think you were wider than me when you proclaimed yourself ready to discuss attributions, influences and other essentially peripheral matter, for the definitions which I have encountered — and they are sprinkled all over everywhere — do attempt to grapple with the nature of the ultimate at closer quarters than that.

The most general of these say that theology is rational talk about God: not logical talk, by the way (for logic would certainly not get you far enough). I like Gerald Priestland's neat dictum, that 'doctrines are not unreasonable certainties, but reasonable uncertainties'. However, even to mention doctrine at this stage is again jumping the gun.

A common strand in present-day definitions is the presence in them of 'experience' — for instance 'reflection on experience'. And I confess that this notion surprised me, but I think I can detect its provenance. Does it not stem from the Hebrew way of conceptualizing God as a God who acts and therefore produces experiences? Whereas our own upbringing, I am sure, rests more heavily on Greek and specifically Platonic modes of thought — much more abstract. At any rate, the introduction of 'experience' into a definition of theology immediately produces the first great divide. Can you study theology if you have not had *any* experience of the matters under discussion? Whose experience counts? Somebody else's, studied analytically: Or are we talking of the arm's length study of the history of the Christian Church? Can an atheist study theology?

I imagine that some years ago the answer to this last question might have been that an atheist can indeed study 'natural' religion, but would find himself unable to stomach 'revealed' religion. (Isn't this somewhat your own position?) Theologians on the whole no longer talk in these terms but we are bidden to familiarize ourselves with the traditional (natural) arguments for the existence of God, not only because of their long and honourable history in philosophical and theological thought, but also to comprehend what it is that present-day thinkers have moved on *from*.

1.   The *ontological* argument for the existence of God was first formulated by Anselm (c. 1033-1109) who to John Hicks was 'the greatest theologian ever to have been Archbishop of Canterbury' (*Philosophy of Religion*. Prentice Hall Inc. 1963 p.15). It can be summarised in his dictum that God is "a being than which nothing greater can be conceived", and long have been the discussions involving Descartes and Kant among others, as to the admissibility of passing from 'conceiving' to 'existing'. Two more recent comments from J.S. Whale and Alan Race himself: Whale: "The mind of man is unintelligible unless mind (God) directs the whole creative process which has brought it to birth" (*Christian Doctrine* CUP 1941 p. 56). Race argues that "the argument claims too much for reason as a process of arguing from the world to God. God cannot be argued to as a matter of fact. Neither can the world. We know the universe by experience; reason and logic can show the relations between existents in the world."

2.   Turning to Thomas Aquinas' five famous proofs for the existence of God, perhaps the most successfully persistent is the *cosmological* argument, to the effect that everything is dependent and thus postulates a necessary being at the end of the chain. "We cannot confess that all our knowledge is relative without thereby betraying our belief in an Absolute which alone gives meaning and measure to relativity. Our knowledge of any event in nature is complete only when the full reason for that event is found in an Ultimate which is its own *raison d'etre*, and which, because it does not depend on anything else, is not of nature but above it." (Whale Ibid.)

3.   A similar form of argument characterises Aquinas's *First Cause* argument: that everything that happens has a cause, and

so on backwards to a First Cause. As Hick points out, the difficulty in this argument lies in excluding as impossible an endless regression. Why not?

4.   The order and design, or *teleological* argument (Aquinas' Fifth Way) has always been highly popular, and still is, despite its logical upsetting by Hume. (*Dialogues concerning Natural Religion.* 1779.) A world so purposefully designed as our own cannot be other than the work of a creative mind, is the argument.

To quote Whale again:

> "The very possibility of science depends on the fact that nature answers to our thought about it, and that our thought answers to nature. Science has to assume as axiomatic the authority of reason and the self-consistency of reality. As obviously reason cannot prove its own authority, one is driven to the conclusion that nature must be itself the work of mind . . ."

The argument surfaced again in one of those Radio 3 late night programmes, in March 1985, in which the strange fact was emphasised, that the universe is intelligible in terms of man-made mathematics.

5.   Aquinas's Fourth Way argues from degrees of value or quality to absolute value or quality. It involves the consciousness of moral obligation towards objective moral values which cannot be explained otherwise than by reference to a transcendant Ground of Values. But to John Hick this very statement begs the question: other philosophers have explained the moral imperative without postulating such a transcendant being.

6.   The last of the Aquinas arguments (as listed here) is in fact his First Way, and seems to have attracted little attention in comparison with the others. It argues from the fact of motion to a Prime Mover, from the processes of change to an initiator of change. The thinking is comparable to that of the First Clause and cosmological arguments it seems to me.

Thus, to recap; the traditional proofs of the existence of God, holed by critics in important respects, yet retain in their modern reformulations elements which I suspect would not be unacceptable to you and to other atheists. It's the Christian revelation you jib at. And it is the Christian theologian's great difficulty to get from the one to the other, to leap over the great divide mentioned earlier. Personally, I find Brian Hebblethwaite's lucid exposition of the dilemma to be valuable (and rendered all the more substantial by having seen him on current TV engaged in high jinks at Queen's, his Cambridge college).

> ". . . Even if God does exist," he writes "he is clearly not accessible to us in the ways in which material objects, living creatures and human being, are. It is this consideration that gives plausibility to the view that God, being Spirit, is accessible only to faith, and that only out of a living relationship to God can the truths of God be known and thought about. A neutral uncommitted approach, on this view, is simply inappropriate to the reality with which theology is concerned" (*The problems of Theology*. C.U.P. 1980 p.14).

Two major Protestant thinkers of this century have devised systems for this inner access to the ultimate reality, Karl Barth (1886-1968) and Rudolf Bultmann (1884-1976). Of course critics have criticised them, as the systems of all philosophers have been criticised down the ages. This is the name of the game. The problems are simply not soluble to human reason when you get to devising a total system. But great thinkers do proffer insights, at the very least, so it is worth while attempting to outline their positions.

Karl Barth, a Swiss Protestant, followed the Danish Kierkegaard (1813-55) in emphasising the 'infinite qualitative distance between God and the world'. And only God, as himself subject, can bridge this gap, never man by will, or by reasoning or by moral behaviour. (The German tradition got very tangled up in logical subject/object concepts.)

Thus all our efforts at reasoning about God (as an object of thought) are not only futile but irreligious. God alone, in his sovereign wisdom can address man and he has chosen to do this in the Incarnation. Man's part is to listen with responsive and obedient attention to this Word of God, who is accomplishing the witness to himself within man and without man doing a thing about it. Certainly not interpreting. Certainly not using historical method or human conceptualization ... The consequence is that God becomes invulnerable; and that the subjective element in all knowledge is discounted to too great a degree.

Rudolf Bultmann's way of access to God was in existential encounter, arrived at by a long process of argument summarised in his 'Jesus Christ and Mythology' (SCM 1958), which I have read and on which I have seven page of notes. From these I attempt my own summary, with quotes!

One has to begin with the impossibility, as he saw it, of the quest for the historical Jesus because of the heavy overlay, and penetration, of mythology.

> "His person is viewed in the light of mythology when he is said to have been Begotten of the Holy Spirit and born of a virgin, and this becomes clearer still in Hellenistic Christian communities where he is understood to be the Son of God in a metaphysical sense, a great pre-existent heavenly being who became man for the sake of our redemption and took on himself suffering, even the suffering of the Cross. It is evident that such conceptions are mythological for they were widespread in the mythologies of Jews and Gentiles and then were transferred to the historical person of Jesus. Particularly the conception of the pre-existent Son of God who descended in human guise into the world to redeem mankind is part of the Gnostic doctrine of redemption, and nobody hesitates to call this doctrine mythological" (pp 16, 17).

I have given this great long extract because it looks very much as if this is the source of all the conflict in the Anglican Church today, with the Bishop of Durham on this side, and his critics on the other. This is pure supposition, by the way, but I can't see that it can be otherwise.

At any rate, this establishment (as Bultmann sees it) of the mythological character of the gospel marks the first step in his argument. The second step is the need to *demythologise*, which he defines not so much as "eliminating the mythological sayings as interpreting them (hermeneutics)". Consider, for instance, the mythological concept of Satan and his armies, a three tiered heaven, earth and hell, and assorted supernatural powers —

> ... "in the modern conception of the world the cause and effect nexus is fundamental ... modern science does not believe that the course of nature can be interrupted, or, so to speak, perforated by supernatural powers." (p. 15)

(Cf York Minster!) But all is not lost. Bultmann believes that myth contains and conceals a still deeper meaning which he proposes to interpret by this demythologising process. (So confusing, this terminology. I keep finding myself inside out, or upside down.) And "to demythologise is to deny that the message of Scripture, and of the Church, is bound to an ancient world view (Weltanschauung) which is obsolete" (Chapeter III). Instead, the message of scripture, the true meaning of God's mystery, lies not in the sphere of theoretical thought but in the sphere of personal existence, he believes.

> "I can understand for example what friendship, love and faithfulness mean and precisely by genuine understanding I know that the friendship, love and faithfulness which I personally enjoy are a mystery which I cannot but faithfully receive. For I perceive them neither by my rational thinking, nor by psychological nor by anthropological analysis but only in open readiness to personal encounters ...
>
> In the same manner I can understand what God's grace means." (p. 43)

Well, there we are. I found Bultmann's first chapters, on myth and demythologising fascinating and largely convincing: but the argument thence to existentialism not so. The consequence, I suspect, for the theological scene as a whole, has been somewhat similar, the destructive side overpowering the constructive side. (But this is supposition again.)

Critics of Bultmann have identified at least two unfortunate consequences — First, the privatisation of a faith whose essence is the reverse of private; and second, inadequate weight accorded to the status and validity of the gospel writings. But it is evident to one that his thought forms the kernel of modern interpretation, however much disputed.

To finish this long long discourse I must comment on your letter of October 25th, in which you say you note 'that theology is an almost entirely *Christian* pre-occupation or indeed obsession and ... attribute this to the fact that the Christian religion begins with, as absolute presuppositions, a set of bizarre assertions . . ." To which I reply that you can hardly pick up a book of *Christian* theology these days without finding yourself referred to Hindu, Tao, Jewish and Islamic counterparts. And secondly, as a matter of verifiable historical fact Christian doctrine does not *begin* with 'absolute presuppositions'. The creeds were drawn up, in sweat and tears, long after the event, to encapsulate the experience of Jesus himself, of disciples, apostles, evangelists and the whole early church. The experience came first, credal formulations later, in modes of thought culturally affected as is all human thought, and therefore ripe for re-interpretation in each succeeding generation (*Pace* Barth *and* Bultmann).

I must stop, and take 3 lb. bags of windfall Bramleys to be sold at our MIND stall on Wednesday. There may not be time to deal with your questions 2 and 3 — nature of Jehovah, and the 'whole package' — before we lunch next Tuesday, to which as always I much look forward.

All love, Nancy

12 November 1985

Dear Nancy,

Thanks for the latest budget; very interesting, promising, encouraging, etc.

But I don't even agree with your first page. I fear I'm a terrible burden to you. I nodded sagely when I read 'I think you were wiser . . .' etc. But when I looked again it said 'I think you were wider!' (i.e. of the mark). Well, save the mark, that's not my view exactly.

We agree that theology is rational talk about God, or the divine or the like. We agree that talk about attributions, dates and so forth is rational (though I *deny* absolutely that it is *peripheral,* as you say). We agree that *logical* talk is rational (though I deny that it can be held *a priori* not to go far enough — that means you've already decided something or other in advance of the projected investigation).

But then at some stage — the next, so far as I can see, without intermission or intermediary, we come to Christian theology, which is, I am sure, quite irrational, because it takes for granted that a supernatural (i.e. irrational) religion, a whole supermarket full of incredible merchandise, is worth talking about. Why should anyone buy any of it?

The 'proofs' of God you mention are Christian proofs, i.e. you have to begin by believing them. It's not a *coincidence,* surely that they all seem to derive from Thomas Aquinas? Watch out: This is not Christian but *Catholic* theology! You'll be travelling to Rome instead of Florence.

I'm sure, on the other hand, that you're right about Bultmann, who surely had to be a Protestant theologian. Of course he's the father in God (alias Nobodaddy) or guru of the Bishop of Durham. And it may well be that there's a great new spiritual resurgence yet to emerge from Christian Existentialism (which gives us much more common ground, by the way, because Kierkegaard, rather admired by me, is literature, a field in which I reckon to be less recalcitrant and more cooperative). This seems to me a likely and lively line to take. However: won't Christians feel that too much truth has been sacrificed, and won't atheists, humanists, etc. feel that too much nonsense remains? If there were good firm ground for an acceptable synthesis, or even a meeting place, this approach could be most rewarding. The practical problem as I see it would be, as regards Christian New Testament belief, why any of it should, or why all of it shouldn't, be demythologised.

Perhaps you're about to found a whole new movement with

something in it for everyone, the persuading of all persuasions. Suggested title: The Complete Mythconception.

Love as ever, E.

23 November 1985.

Dear Nancy,

Of course you're right in saying that my methodology is not clearly applicable, even inimical, to *theology*. But it's all I can do. I've always been impressed by the legend of Le Jongleur de Notre Dame: all that otherwise maladroit and untalented monk could do was juggle, so he juggled to the point of agonised exhaustion before a statue of Our Lady, who duly desceneded from her plinth and wiped his brow. There may be a general rule of equilibrium, that all our strengths are by the same token our weaknesses, since it takes so long to be good at anything that there is no time left to excel at anything else, so that we pay for our little knowledge by a lot of compulsory ignorance. But I needn't say all that, because you know it already: and the limitations of the method when applied to theology are already well known to you. However, I must add that I do share at least one precept with the injunctions of scripture namely whatsoever thy hand findeth to do, do it with all thy might — and the rest of that melancholy and moving utterance.

Love, yours E.

January 20, 1986

Otterbourne

My dear E,

Lovely to see you and in basically bubbling form.

My own literary progress has been nil. B. has had 'flu or whatever the present virus is — her normally robust defences being at a low ebb after cortisone et al. And what is a cough? Recurrence of lung cancer or operation of virus? So once again I've been over there giving general support of a rather ill-defined kind, but so timed that it's just *impossible* to sit down and write anything. Hence frustration. Though I wouldn't *NOT*. You know the scenario, having gone through it yourself.

So this morning, just to get writing again, I'm going to do an essay on our sheet which requires no scholarship of any description, nor library reference, no nothing, frankly autobiographical and it may be unreadable. At least I've got an hour or two free, and I've lit the fire, and a cigarette, and it's bliss.

Have you heard this definition of an atheist: someone without invisible means of support?

All love as ever, Nancy

January 20, 1986

Otterbourne

Dear E,

A year ago I wrote to you something to the effect that belief in God made to me the most sense of the world and its problems; and wasn't this theology? And you said — no, it isn't theology; more like autobiography.

Well, here comes the autobiography vindicated because it corresponds to one of our optional titles for an essay. Actually it should have been last term, but as I'm not following the set pattern for the diploma, but writing letters to an atheist instead, that won't matter. The title is

"What difference does belief in God make in your experience?" — a real invitation to the waltz.

I begin now, as I began then, with the statement that belief in God makes sense, and that the existence of God as a first cause, and more particularly as the highest value, is a belief which in its modern formulations is still intellectually tenable. Obviously to an academic of any sort it is important to start from a base line which is intellectually satisfying and viable.

Where you go from there, from a first cause to a loving father as revealed in Christianity is the major question which I wrote about last time. But the fact that you have to resort to mystery to account for it — to account for instance for the complete

65

humanity and complete divinity of Jesus — seems to me, curiously, also intellectually satisfying in the sense that life as I know it corresponds more closely to that type of world than to the world of logical tautology.

Bultmann's account of love and friendship, the mysterious interaction between two human beings which he designates as existential, conveys something of this.

But intellectual satisfaction (that the existence of God makes sense, *not* that it can be proved by logical method) is not of first importance in my experience. It is only the *sine qua non* to somebody of my upbringing and at the latter end of life. One has to look back and ask: what about the early years?

First, one has to acknowledge, along with Maurice Wiles, the immense if hidden influence of family upbringing and family, school and national heritage. A Bishop among one's forebears, a parson grandfather, a Quaker grandmother (different families!), a genius of a visionary and unorthodox headmistress, uniquely keen on living life to the full, including sacrificially. It never struck us that Christianity might not be true. Our job was to investigate what particularly it held for us (and vice versa, you understand, for we were idealists as only the young can be) — in fact, though we did not use the word as children, to interpret it. And if we thought, as emotional adolescents, that we ought to be having all sorts of religious experiences but didn't in fact have them, well *tant pis* one wasn't made like that.

But perhaps one was made like that? When I was leaving school at the age of 17 and one week, a deeply religious girl also in the sixth form persuaded me to attend an Oxford Group (MRA) house party with her. That proved emotional, no two ways about it. The fiancée of an R.N. submariner recently drowned was among those who spoke of their belief, and it was immensely moving. This was still peace-time, you must remember.

For a few weeks afterwards I sat on the school's terraced slopes, gazing out over the Berkshire countryside and listening intently for the voice of God, which, as the Moral Rearmers and many others have believed, would come directly to me. (At this stage I knew nothing of schizophrenia and religious mania and hallucinations). . . . What happened? The fact remains that, a few months later, in the finishing school which was to launch us as debs. for a London season, I suddenly announced that I wished to be prepared for Somerville College entrance. (Hitherto, to the uncomprehending exasperation of my aforesaid headmistress, I had steadfastly refused to contemplate a university career.) To the credit of my astonished teachers and tutors, all was made possible. Instead of court curtseys, Dante's Purgatorio, taught in Italian by an impassioned Florentine spinster. Instead of the life of the middle-class deb., the challenges of university-level thinking and all it could lead to: fifty years ago this was still very much a minority option for girls.

So it could be said that belief in God, sparked off and given motivating force by emotional M.R.A. encounters, did in fact re-direct one's whole life. I may not, in fact *have* not, achieved anything much but I am convinced that without a degree and the opportunity to know one's fellow undergraduates, I would have achieved a very great deal less.

Latterly, belief in God has I think made one much braver than when young. I'm not talking about galloping over the countryside, or ski-ing down a mountain, or swimming quite long distances, all of which were possible in those halcyon days. Rather, I think I mean the freedom to meet, and feel one can cope with, all sorts of people. I mean the knowledge that one can speak at quite large conferences (and have something to say). That one is enabled somehow to carry on, and mean something to people as they mean a great deal to me, despite bereavement and the torturing uncertainty of cancer in the family. If you check up that what you are doing, or proposing to do, is at least consistent with the will of God so far as you can judge (supposing there *is* a God and that he *has* a will, for one never *knows*), then a deep peace descends.

The orthodox dogmatic will remark that in this entire recital this particular believer makes no mention of sin. Ideas of atonement and salvation simply do not register, though of course one learns about them and indeed recites the creeds containing them at every church service. Salvation is a particular *bête noir*: it smacks so of calculated egotism as an objective and surely urgently needs re-definition, de-mythologising and the whole modern treatment! I never give the Ten Commandments a second thought but rely entirely on Jesus' love commandment, more than enough for anyone. The one sin I pray to avoid is: not to be doing enough, or being enough: not to be disciplined enough, lest when a moment arrives to give crucial help, one is asleep, or unfit, or overindulged. Insensitive. Unaware. Even soft, offering soft options for the sake of a quiet life.

For when I think about it, I am conscious of a thousand blessings, national and personal, physical and mental. And from those to whom much is given, much also will be required. Another sobering thought, that like so many of us, I fear, one is altogether too temperate, and sober, and as John Taylor said, bland as a Christian.

27 January 1986

Dear Nancy,

Thanks for your letter and enclosure. Yes, I entirely understand how you are now placed; I've been there too. And in many ways stayed there, and always shall. If an account were made, totting up hours and minutes spent, like a civil service organisation and methods study, I wonder how much of one's waking life would be spent in just doing one's best under difficult circumstances? Under that rubric I'm ready also to subsume e.g. writing whatever books one has it in one to write. It's all somehow the same essential activity: latent or realised energy being acted upon by external forces and events. The description applies equally, come to think of it, to the planets in their orbits and the stars in their courses. Even though the sun might long to lie in, it has to rise; the starry firmament yearns in vain for an early night. The trick is to combine compulsory activity with a relaxed feeling of self indulgence. I seem to manage that all right. Too well, even.

Now to the latest epistle to the Croydonians. The first thing I want to wonder about God is why people who believe and who disbelieve in him/her/it are so strikingly similar, quite often: go

68

to the same schools, and read the same books, stay tremendous *chums*. It seems so strange that so cosmic a differenc should make so little difference (so far as I can see) in standards, attitudes, comportment and so forth. It's exactly as if (dis)believing in God were just one way of dis(believing) in God, and conversely. And he/she/it doesn't seem to make any clear distinction either. Not only rain but tidal waves and oceans of molten lava fall indifferently on the just and unjust, theist and atheist alike. Which reminds me that while I entirely feel the force of that merry quip about the atheist as a person without invisible means of support, I want to enquire why that isn't just as true, if not so amusing, about the *theist*?

Either way — *what* support, exactly? Very well, then, on my own showing the central thesis is indeed the one to which you address yourself: what difference does belief in God make in your experience? And the answer I confidently expect you to reach, and indeed demonstrate is, in a word, *none*.

And this despite an early conditioning that could hardly be more disparate. No bishops or curates even among any of my forebears: just sailors, shepherds, smugglers, fiddlers, and essentially farm labourers, who all hated the parson and the squire with equal fervour. It never for a single second occurred to any of us, after the age of about eight or nine, that Christianity might be true. Christmas and Father Christmas lost their little adherents at about the same time, and for much the same reason; nice stories but not true.

Nobody even hoped that, à la Hardy, it might be so: The whole basic cast of mind of the peasant class, world wide, is utterly unChristian and perpetually pagan, from paganus (a-um) rustic. It's no coincidence that the last witch in England was burnt in rural Essex, and rather recently too. I never had the least doubt that she looked exactly like (and indeed probably was) my grandmother.

Yet from this utterly pagan and secular background I've done and thought and said and experience, in ordinary terms, much the same as you: and indeed some at least of that experience has been joyfully shared, I hope to our mutual enrichment: certainly to mine. There seem to be no barriers to our understanding and reciprocation.

So I have to ask again: why introduce an unknown x when the equation already balances? If the concept of God makes such a difference to you, why has it never made any difference at all to me (for example)?

I can see though that it helps your prose style. It is (isn't it? just as I said) autobiography, but it's personally very persuasive, even powerful, as a piece of prose. If God can help people to write well, he/she/it serves a good purpose, which could with benefit be extended to theologians generally. They so often seem to write so diabolically!

Love as ever, E.

28.1.86

My dear E,

God as Jehovah

Continuing the attempt to pick up the loose ends of our previous correspondence, I turn to your second heading, God as Jehovah: or, as you put it in your letter of December 9, 1984:

> "I'm perfectly sure that you may not pick and choose among testaments to suit yourself. The God of Christianity is the God of the Old Testament, never doubt that. You accept or reject the package."

I see I sent a reply exactly a year ago to the day but I think it needs expanding. It certainly didn't satisfy you then. So here we go again.

In last year's lectures on the New Testament, it was pointed out that the relationship between the Old Testament and the New has been regarded in three different ways. First, that the message of the New Testament breaks so much new ground, is so entirely novel, that it owes nothing of essential significance to its O.T. antecedent. Jesus proclaimed a covenant involving a break with history so complete that all subsequent events in the western world have been dated from his birth (albeit a shade erroneously). The second veiwpoint is that the O.T. and the N.T. form a continuum, that the God of the O.T. is the God of the

70

N.T., and those holding this view, such as yourself point to the fact that Jesus was a Jew, that he taught in the synagogues, and that Christianity was at first regarded as a sect within Judaism. All Jesus' sayings which you quote are adduced in support of this viewpoint. It is even believed that Jesus never conceived of himself as preaching beyond Jewry.

Recent television programmes have homed in on this (admittedly close) relationship between Jewry (O.T.) and Christianity (N.T.) and talk of Judaeo-Christianity. In so doing, they may well be correcting a tendency to pay too little attention to Jewry, for I think it must have formed little part of the muscular missionary Anglo-saxon Christianity of our grandfathers, which percolated through to us as children.

If Christianity is regarded as a deviant sect of Judaism and Jesus simply as a prophet like Old Testament prophets, then Islam too would go along with that and indeed it is a stance adopted by some low Christologists in the debate about the relationship between faiths. But evidently this can not be the Christianity to whom the Incarnation is a tenet of the faith.

The third view is that Jesus, while fulfilling the promise of the Old Testament, transformed it so that it became a new religion. In your words, you accept the package but by the time it reaches you it is no longer the same package. As Alan Race commented in his lecture a fortnight ago, "Christianity interpreted the Messianic age differently from Jewish expectations when it incorporated the suffering of Jesus theme so centrally in its understanding. This is why it can be said that Christianity is a new religion, and not simply the fulfilment of Judaism." In the words of the communion service "On these two commandments (i.e. to love God and your neighbour as yourself) hang all the law and the prophets."

The theme can be elaborated if we turn (with some relief) to a bit of historical narrative in which it seems to me to be possible to pinpoint the period when the momentous change occurred. Undoubtedly of course in one sense the *actual* occasion was the preaching, death and resurrection of Jesus. But its effect could only take place when it was apprehended by somebody. And as so often, that somebody was Paul.

71

The passage in question is Acts 15: 1-35, in which Paul's meeting with the Council in Jerusalem is described. Because of her clear grasp of the issues involved, the commentary of the distinguished N.T. scholar Morna Hooker is quoted at some length below.

... "The question of Gentile admission to the Church had apparently been settled in Acts 11: 18. Yet here we find Jewish Christians still arguing that Gentile converts to Christianity must accept the same obligations as Gentile converts to Judaism: i.e., they must be circumcised and they must keep the Jewish law ...

It is not surprising that the problem took long to solve.

... "It must have seemed entirely logical to the majority of Jewish Christians that Gentiles who accepted Jesus as the Jewish Messiah should become Jewish proselytes in the normal way. Once Gentiles were admitted without the requirement that they must submit to circumcision and obey the Jewish law, it was impossible to contain the Christian community within Judaism: the Christian community began to be seen as a new movement, rather than simply the fulfilment of Jewish hopes ...

The admission of Gentiles on equal terms was therefore a momentous step ... There is no doubt that it changed the character of Christianity ...

(Hooker. *Studying the New Testament*. p. 128)

In other words; for quite some time these earliest followers were unsure whether the God they worshiped possessed Judaistic characteristics demanding circumcision etc.; or new testament characteristics demanding faith in Christ. When the latter view prevailed, the nature of the package changed.

All the above, nevertheless, to me needs supplementing by considerations of epistemology, or theory of knowledge, which would account for the very different perceptions, conceptions, and ideas of the nature of God at different times and places. These considerations relate to a much more fundamental level of perception than the 'historical determinist' considerations.

Hope to write something on this next.

Love Nancy.

My dear E,

In my last letter about *God as Jehovah* I threatened you with a tail-piece or coda. My whole account struck me as incomplete and in need of shoring up by reference to the philosophical problem of epistemology, the theory of knowledge. How does anybody know anything? What we have been talking about is not the nature of God himself, for nobody knows this (other than what Jesus taught which for practical purposes suffices): it is what men and women in divers times and in divers places have thought to be the nature of God; and the transition from one belief to the next.

Since the Enlightenment biblical scholarship has fastened on this idea of cultural determinism, the viewing of each scriptural episode and writing dispassionately in its own setting; and, it has to be said, providing thereby incalculably important insights. It accounts, for instance, for regarding the jealous God of the Old Testament who slew entire armies and made full use of the dirty tricks department as the view of the nomadic tribe of our earlier correspondence. And also, with many a birth-pang and largely due to Paul, for the New Testament view of the same God. The clear play of subjective perception, surely.

But what I want to touch on here is the more fundamental epistemological question: "How do we know anything?" which takes us from Exodus to the contemporary complexities of modern physics. Actually "touch on" is the operative phrase, because I am barely capable of recapping student essays on empiricism *versus* idealism, Locke and Hume *versus* Bp. Berkeley and so forth: even if this were the right place. But the jump to Kant is important, for it was he who insisted on the perceiver's contribution required to make sense of the raw data of perception. For those of us who are not mystics (and perhaps they are taken care of by Karl Barth or the existentialists?) this input by the perceiver is essential, as I see it.

Continuing the theme, suppose we see how it works out when applied to scientific knowledge, its supposed certainties so often set up in opposition to religious knowledge to the disparagement of the latter. I am a total non-scientist but believe two common-sense points may be made as a start.

First, scientific knowledge is not 'certain' but a series of hypotheses. The philosopher Karl Popper was a great exponent of this truth. Each hypothesis lasts until supplanted by the next: Galileo, Newton, Einstein, quantum mechanics and the physics of atomic and sub-atomic particles. There seems to be nothing fixed about it. The laws form a series or progression as apprehended by successive geniuses: or sometimes geniuses making simultaneous advances in a 'ripe' climate, so to speak. But the climate doesn't make the advance. Minds do.

Second: this same scientific knowledge does not come to us, sense-perception-wise, as to a *tavola rasa*(?) You need a human mind to categorise it, and before and after you need the whole apparatus of scientific paraphenalia either to observe it, by space-probe, camera, telescope or microscope; or to calculate its properties (by computer). You do this by the application of man-made mathematics, which, lo and behold, at the end of the day, corresponds to the data provided by the universe. The input of the human mind for sorting all this out is indispensable.

I think all this is so obvious that nobody bothers to mention it.

But now we come to more abstruse matters. I was fascinated on Sunday night (January 26, 1986) by a programme on physics and mysticism featuring a Dr. Fritzof Capra of Berkeley, California.

Apparently when you get to atomic physics the following statements may be made:

(i)   It is impossible to know the position and velocity of an atom simultaneously.

(ii)   It is not certain that a sub-atom is anything more than an idea, a mental construct.

(iii) Atomic and sub-atomic particles are best described not as matter but as inter-relationship. And here they showed a scary picture of rather Heath Robinson relationships forever changing pattern and plane and generally chasing each other around.

74

From here Dr. Capra somehow jumped to Chinese Tao mysticism, whither I could not follow him in any sense. Nor does this seem necessary.

For within the Christian tradition one is immediately reminded of John Taylor's book *The Go Between God*, in which he interprets the operation of the Holy Spirit in ways intelligible to contemporary understanding. I must not push the analogy too far and it may be that I am now talking nonsense. A confusion of atoms does not equate with the Holy Spirit. But can it be that the raw stuff of the universe, and of its creator, should be regarded as a matter of relationships?

These last few paragraphs are a diversion. What I have been mainly trying to show is that the input of the perceiver, even at its most basic and elementary level, is a pre-requisite for knowledge of any sort, including scientific knowledge. This input is only subjective in the sense that it is provided by the perceiver: it need not vitiate the 'objectivity' of what is observed (which is an illusion anyhow in the sense that it is continually re-defined and re-interpreted).

If this is the case for science, why not so for religion, knowledge about God and knowledge of God? In this respect religion is no worse off than science. Both systems are apprehended by the human mind when certain pre-requisites are fulfilled.

Thus 'experience' is vindicated. And as Archbishop Ramsay said: "I can't see how you can have experience unless it is of something."

Love Nancy

P.S. Just got your letter of 27 January, for which so very many thanks. An amusing yet profound re-statement of one of my original problems: no barriers to our understanding and reciprocation yet one a believer and the other not. Are we on the way to solving this one, I wonder?

1 February 1986

Dear Nancy,

Thanks for your latest instalment, again delightfully lively in style though taut and trim in topic and treatment. But I still stumble at the same blocks. The fact that Paul said O.K., Gentiles can have N.T. Christianity, is surely what *proves* that this was a Jewish religion? How, otherwise, could the question ever have arisen?

It's not a bit of use pretending that the incarnation is a Christian invention or addition. It obviously belonged to, and was an integral part of, Paul's Jewish faith, which he began by preaching to his fellow-Jews, some of whom accepted it, long before the Gentile question arose. As to 'it is even believed that Jesus never conceived of himself as preaching beyond Jewry', I suppose that is believed because Jesus himself said so, which seems to me a *good* reason. Cf. Matthew 15: 24.

I'm sorry, but even without circumcision that talk about abstaining from blood and things strangled still makes me feel like an eavesdropper in some disgusting madhouse. It is apparently applied to the Gentiles, but I for one want no part of it. I'm not all that keen on the incarnation either, which I see as either meaningless or blasphemous. Among a heaving ocean of religious doubt I have a rock-like certainty about one thing, and one only: the creator of the universe, if there is such an entity, was certainly never made flesh, any more that it was made toffee or India rubber, or sealing wax, or Gorgonzola cheese.

Love E.

15 February 1986

Dear Nancy,

Here are a few tweaks to the tailpiece.

1.   It's TABULA RASA.

2.   The uncertainty principle you mention dates from before I was born, I think.

3.   If Dr. Capra *really* believes that matter *really* consists solely of rational interrelationships I'm not surprised he jumped into Chinese mysticism; he seems to be headed straight for the loony-bin. Don't try to follow him.

4.   I'm quite sure it's *not true* that science is just a series of different arbitrary hypotheses. Beyond doubt, there is progress in scientific knowledge. The obvious measure of it is technology. TV and space probes *work* because of improved theoretical knowledge and understanding: we live longer because doctors *know* more, in terms of simple fact.

5.   I don't recognise Kant from your description of him. I'm sure he said nothing so simple as the dictum you attribute to him (the perceiver makes sense of sense-data). I mean, could there ever have been any philosopher who didn't see that, just for starters? Of course human beings perceive and infer in human terms, with human equipment: what else? Am I missing something?

6.   What's interesting, though, is the limits of knowledge. If you're talking about theology at all, you've already gone beyond *my* limits.

7.   If you can link the feet on the ground viewpoint with the head-in-the-clouds viewpoint, that will be a great achievement. But how is it to be done?

Love as ever, E.

Otterbourne

February 19/24, 1986

My dear E,

Many thanks for your tweaks to my tail-piece dated February 15th. I hasten to deal with these — and I really do mean deal — before passing on to another major subject: Salvation — Atonement — Liberation — all in one breath.

1.   Thanks for TABULA RASA.

2.   I don't recognise the uncertainty principle I am supposed to have mentioned before you were born. Thought I was being unusually certain, for me.

3.   It isn't only Dr. Capra. I came in and switched on half way through another TV discussion on molecules and such, and found that a very sane-looking professor of some sort of physics

from Newcastle on Tyne was talking much the same language. His own method of epistemology was to construct models (what else?) and see how they fitted.

4.   You wickedly insert the word 'arbitrary' into my script. Of course there is progress, for each innovator builds on the shoulders of his predecessor and at the operational level technology succeeds. No argument between us there. And no doubt Newton himself thought that he had spoken the last word. But, lo and behold again, Newtonian physics, which is abstruse enough for the likes of me, has been superseded by Einstein for starters, and now we're even in the post-Einstein era. And it takes someone like Karl Popper to point out what has been going on. I understand that some philosophers of science now talk of the *relativity* of scientific statements.

5.   Over to Kant with a new paragraph. He wrote a great deal, and may be you are not familiar with the *Critique of Pure Reason*, in which, if I remember rightly, he worked out, in a very far from simple way, how the perceiver imposes categories on data received. And what I wrote was not a dictum of Kant as you (again wickedly) state. It was a short hand summary. Of course human beings operate in human terms: but how? The subject is still a very open one, and constituted last year's Reith Lectures on the relationship between brain and mind and the universe. It seems to me that a lot of the subject matter of previous generations of philosophers has been taken over by scientists, particularly physicists, and that there is a mind-boggling area where philosophy, theology and physics meet.

6. and 7. I'm finding increasingly that the theological books I am now reading do in fact go way beyond the limits of the theological enterprise which we more or less agreed at the beginning. They have to, if they are to deal with contemporary questioning and not get stuck two thousand years ago. The great point about Christianity is that the Christ-event (a phrase I detest but which here seems inescapable) marked a beginning and not an end. And all this represents the current heads-in-the-clouds aspect while previous generations speculated in terms of angels, demons, platonic souls etc. The feet-on-the-ground aspect is represented by the concept of liberation-theology,

which will figure in the next essay.

Atonement — Salvation — Liberation

I have been thinking about these for weeks, in fact longer, because it was what amounted to the doctrine of Atonement that we wrote to each other about last year. You jibbed at "a religion of guilt, sin, redemption, blood, hellfire, flagellation and general torture all round which seems to (you) just a form of lunacy, and a peculiarly vicious and repugnant form at that . . ." and at "the God who was *satisfied* by the crucifixion" (23 November 1984). For my part, I kept informing my tutors, passionately if ignorantly, that I could not do with salvation, which struck me as grossly egotistical and not to be compared with the altruism of the World Wildlife Fund.

In any event, one of the optional essay titles this term is "What do you understand by the term — salvation?" and this came as a golden opportunity to go into the whole subject: clearly there must be more to it than one first thought. Theologians may be difficult but they're not dumb. And so often problems turn out to be problems of linguistics, because language needs continual updating when outmoded terms no longer ring any bells.

So off I went to the Lyttleton Library in the Close at Winchester to see if they had got any of the books on our list, and great was my delight at finding a paperback of only 100 pages (SCM 1982) by Frances Young, a Methodist and lecturer at the Birmingham University Theological faculty. Its title *"Can these dry bones live?"* tells one nothing but otherwise I found it splendid — learned, but easy to read, deeply thought through but blessedly unsanctimonious. I can do no better than to summarise her main points, with full acknowledgment. She came as quite a revelation. And I guess she did the same thing for Alan Race, who I find based some of his lecture upon her.

First the history. Anselm (c. 1033-1109) whom we have met before, wrote *Cur Deus Homo?*, why did God become Man? of which the thesis is that man cannot be saved without satisfaction for sin, for justice required that sin be punished, and Jesus alone — God alone — was capable of this *satisfaction*. The debt is so great. "So the incarnation becomes a logical necessity for the resolution of man's problems": Christ satisfied the

79

abstract principle of justice. (This is evidently where the concept of satisfaction comes in, very different from how it struck you.)

This theory penetrated deeply, was taken up by John Bunyan, and has remained the faith of conservative churchmen both catholic and evangelical ever since (cf. C.S. Lewis): It is known technically as the Penal Substitution theory.

Paul Tillich, a noted theologian, has pointed out the strong psychological effect it can induce, despite its dated legalistic terminology and its quantitative measuring of sin and punishment. And Frances Young herself testifies, as part of her evangelical experience, to the relief and freedom of realising that reponsibility for one's failures has been lifted.

But this does not prevent her from posing the awkward questions which Anselm's view invites: viz.,

1.   It makes unsatisfactory law: too inequitable.

2.   It makes God bound or determined by an abstract principle of justice.

3.   It damages trinitarian theology, setting the Father and the Son against each other.

4.   Above all, it was originally *not scripturally based* but legally based, although scripture has subsequently been adduced in aid.

The second theory was put forward by Abelard (1079-1142), famous for his original and independent thinking in relation to the Atonement as well as for his love of Héloise immortalised by Helen Waddell. To him, "the cross was a demonstration of God's love and grace: this demonstration called forth our repentance so that we could be forgiven and return to obedience to God's will . . . Abelard refuses to accept that God was offered to the devil as a ransom-price; nor does he like the idea that he is offered to God either . . . Repentance is produced by contemplation of the cross; love in generated in us in response to God's demonstration of love on the cross."

The common criticism of this theory is that it is too subjective. All it effects is man's response to God's act of love . . . The cross did not make any objective difference to the situation. But Frances Young thinks this is no bad thing, for over-emphasis on the cross leads to all sorts of difficulties. "What about people before the event?" (One of your points too.) And even, what about Jesus' acts of forgiveness given during his life-time before the crucifixion?

Broadly speaking, it seems that positions on the Atonement have become polarised in accordance with these two opposing views of Anselm (conservative churchmanship) and Abelard (liberal).

Into this situation a third scholar, the Swede, Gustaf Aulen, in the early 1930s dropped a kind of star wars solution of God *versus* the Devil which was said to go back to the Church Fathers. What they — the Church Fathers — were deeply aware of was the fact that man's problem is not just sin, a moral problem, as the Western approaches to atonement tend to assume. Rather more is something in the present constitution of creation as a whole which is corrupt. Sin is one symptom of a deeper problem which includes ignorance, powerlessness, decay and death.

Aulen's ideas took effect, for Liberalism was receiving a nasty shock from Nazism in the 1930s and 40s. Evil was evidently rempant, and people were much more aware of it.

As to how the whole of God's creation could become corrupt, Frances Young quotes a memorable passage of Simone Weil's, which I repeat.

"The creation is an abandonment. In creating what is other than himself, God necessarily abandoned it . . .

Because he is the creator, God is not all-powerful. Creation is abdication. But he is all-powerful in this sense, that his abdication is voluntary. He knows its effects and wills them . . . God has emptied himself. This means that both the Creation and the Incarnation are included with the Passion.

The apparent absence of God in this world is the actual reality of God"

p. 57, from *Selected pensées of Simone Weil*, quoted in *Gateway to God*, ed. Raper. Fontana 1974.

Finally, Frances Young finds no one solution adequate on its own.

The meaning of the words

Frances Young points out that the language describing the Atonement is that of the law-courts and the battlefield, the social institution of slavery and the religious practice of sacrifice. The first two are still with us, the last two are not. Efforts of imagination are therefore required to take on board the jargon relating to slavery and sacrifice no longer practised in our society. She therefore initiates a penetrating enquiry into the meaning of probably the key word in relation to the Atonement, the Greek word *Hilasterion*. Does it mean propitiation, as expounded by Lear Morris (a theologian I've never heard of) or expiation, as held by C.H. Dodd and the liberals?

"The early Christians", she wrote "proclaimed that Christ died for our sins, that Christ Jesus was *hilasterion* through faith in his blood."

Precisely how such expressions are to be interpreted lies at the heart of the liberal-conservative controversy. The conservative (again, cf Lewis), understands them to mean that Christ's blood was shed in payment of the penalty properly exacted for our sin by God's righteousness, to propitiate the entirely justified wrath of God at our sinfulness, and so reconcile us to the Holy One we had offended . . .

The liberal wants to give a very different exegesis, emphasising the love and mercy of God rather than his wrath and judgment."

For her part, Frances Young finds something to be said for both sides, viz:

That Morris rightly draws attention to the wrath and judgment of God as the biblical context in which these words are used; Greek speakers will certainly have understood *hilasterion* as propitiation, as did the Greek Fathers of the Church. On the other hand Dodd was right to point out that God does not in the Bible generally appear as the recipient of an offering or sacrifice but as *providing* it as subject. (Romans 3:25),

"The people did not offer bribes to buy off God's anger; indeed, the prophets condemned those who thought they could get away with that kind of thing. Rather, God in his mercy provided the sacrificial system for his people so that sin could be dealt with and the covenant kept in being. In the time of the New Testament, it seems to have been generally assumed that the sacrifices were to be offered simply *because God commanded them*, and the Epistle to the Hebrews suggests that their purpose was regarded as purifactory and nothing else." (Heb. 9:22) (p. 70.)

The sequel: Extending the concept of sacrifice in the light of the foregoing.

The meaning of the atonement has been seriously distorted by unscholarly assumptions of the nature and purpose of sacrifice, concentrating too much on the problem of sin, and suggesting that sacrifice is some kind of compensation for it. Further, our present culture is one which no longer utilises and understands the nature of cultic sacrifice.

To elaborate: in the world in which the Church grew up, religion without sacrifice was unthinkable. Indeed, since the Christians did not practise sacrifice, they rapidly became known as atheists! . . . Sacrifice was the unquestioned method of facilitating communion with the divine. In time, sacrifice almost equated with worship, and worship with sacrifice. And the different elements of worship, communion, praise, thanksgiving, homage, sin-offering, all had their sacrificial counterparts.

Where does all this get us? Never one to shirk the issue, Frances Young advances a synthesis and a solution: All aspects of sacrifice are taken up together and culminate in Christ's sacrifice so that a wholly new situation and relationship with God (salvation, I suppose) is created. A new covenant is sealed with his blood (as all covenants were sealed with blood).

The place to look for this in the Bible is the Epistle to the Hebrews, incidentally *not* written by Paul. The old prophetic criticisms of sacrifice were right: God did not want that sort of worship but the sacrifice of complete obedience, total self-offering, which was what Christ gave. And turning to Paul:

83

To present your bodies as a living sacrifice, holy and acceptable to God, which is your spiritual worship. (Rom. 12:1.)

To Frances Young, everything now falls into place. Atonement is necessary because the very act of creation implies allowing the creation autonomy, God abandoning his creation to be itself . . . Christs' sacrifice was neither a bribe to buy off God's anger, nor just an expression of God's love for us. It was the mutual participation of God and man in a costly effort to reintegrate what had been torn assunder.

(A.R. Taking responsibility for creating a world where evil exists, and providing a means by which God can be found in suffering and death-dealing experiences. But after Auschwitz, even this is stretching things.)

Well, there we are. I must say I find it illuminating, as always, to see a problem presented in its historical setting: But this is not the end of it for me, for the doctrine of the atonement is that Christ's sacrifice, explained as above, brings about our salvation, and it is the word salvation which has always turned me off.

The last place where this occurred was, you may remember, in my autobiographical essay. "Salvation", I wrote "smacks so of calculated egotism and surely urgently needs re-definition, de-mythologising and the whole modern treatment." Alongside, in his red ink, Alan Race wrote "Try speaking of *liberation* at many levels", and again this has been an absolute revelation, a wholly new idea which I have never heard uttered in many years of church-going.

I don't know how many levels this will work out at: on the personal level (the least important) the bells are already ringing. But all this happened to coincide with our scheduled lecture on Liberation theology, and also with a quick visit to Church House where the Archbishop of Canterbury and David Shepherd were talking about the report "Faith in the City". My original idea was to carry straight on melding the three key words of my title into one thesis. But events have again overtaken me.

I'll be in touch. All love, Nancy.

Dear Nancy,

Many thanks for your last: much food for thought, as usual.

The uncertainty principle you mentioned was Heisenberg's: we can measure *either* the position or the velocity of a particle. I take this to concern the nature of measurement, not the nature of reality. Personally I wouldn't be too disturbed about the differences between Newtonian and Einsteinian physics. Does anyone seriously dispute the main outlines of either? Again the questions are those of the validity of experimental measurements, aren't they? Nor am I disposed to be sidetracked by the demotion of physical science to mere technology. The mere functional existence of space probes proves (from Latin probo?) that the relevant theoretical physics and astronomy has actually been mastered, in terms of understood and realised scientific principles. Popper is all very well: but Popper couldn't even have given us the zip fastener.

Of course it's entirely legitimate for scientists themselves to debate what their knowledge actually means: and in such a debate logicians are entitled to intervene (as Susan Stebbing did in the similar perplexities of the 1930s). But I'm sure it won't do for the rest of us to infer that there is some deep quasi-theistic mystery at the heart of the universe which somehow pops up in the supposed gap between Newton and Einstein. A simple explanation seems to be that there are difficult and technical topics, about which philosophical and epistemological perplexities are not unpredictable.

You're quite right in saying that I'm unfamiliar with *Die Kritik der reinen Vernunft*, as indeed I have been ever since I first studied it as required reading for the Cambridge tripos. But again I can't feel that the Kantian depths and difficulties about the nature of perception somehow in themselves justify Christian *Theology*, any more than conceptual difficulties about practical physics. I don't think that we can hope to prove very much by way of an appeal to what we don't understand.

I'm still jibbing at salvation. Let me try to formulate my problems more precisely. First — just what exactly is it that I and the rest of femina/homo sapiens have been guilty *of*, or atoned *for*, or redeemed *from*? And secondly what difference exactly, has been made in practice by all this atonement redemption, precious blood, etc? How would anything or anyone, anywhere, be otherwise than it now is, in any significant respect, if these universe-shattering redemptions etc. had simply never occurred at all? — as indeed for the more than massive majority of humanity, over the last 5 million years or so, and for all other faiths in the last 2000, they have not.

Well, pending the reply, I surely should read some Frances Young (though her title surely must be Shall these bones live?).

Off the train now and into the pub and the stupefying clamour of pop muzak. But at least I have a surface to write on, a firm basis for discourse and commentary.

That's far more than I'm able to say about the topic of atonement etc. which seems to inspire you but continues to leave me utterly bewildered. It might just as well be in Sanskrit. It's certainly nothing I can recognise as Sams-script. How did God ever come to have this mad obsession with blood? It seems to me that he's the one who needs the redemption, or at least some form of treatment. Perhaps revulsion-therapy would help. Meanwhile I feel that the covenant had better get back into the ark where it belongs, and leave ordinary people in peace.

Well, you must explain it all to me when we meet. I infer from the vivacity of your prose that you've found something; as when on Southend pier in my long vanished youth the anglers' bells and lines set up a sudden excitement. But there was often a catch in it in quite the wrong sense.

Love as ever, E.

25 July 1986

Dear Nancy,

Thanks for yours. I thought you might like the enclosed *TLS* page. Everything it says strikes me as utter gibberish. But there does seem to emerge a glimmering of definition; belief means that one knows everything without evidence and theology means that with evidence no one knows anything. Belief gives everyone different certainties; theology, the same uncertainty. The latter conveys an illusion of communion or sharing, which makes it very popular. But all that is actually being held in common, it seems to me, is confusion. I hope you're going to clear all this up. When the time is ripe, that is.

Love as ever, E.

9 August 1986

Dear Nancy,

. . . What I noticed was that you mentioned that you had made no mention of theology: So it's not far from the surface of consciousness if not central among your active preoccupations. I had a theological thought yesterday, namely that whatever powers that be happen to prevail now must presumably be the same governing body or bodies that have been in operation since the big bang and before, if there was a before. Some vast number of billions of years, at the last count. There's surely something very odd about the idea of a new force injected into time at the last tick of the cosmic clock? The same rules of procedure must surely govern homo sapiens so called as our predecessors in the animal vegetable and mineral kingdom? It's easy to exaggerate the importance of our species, let along our feelings as individuals. Time, that takes survey of all the world, must have a stop. Give context, and discuss.

Love as ever, E.

19 August 1986

Dear Nancy,

I enclose the latest Longley, in case you hadn't seen it. The Bishop of Durham seemed to address the General Synod as if he had strayed into a madhouse, and was received as if he had strayed out of one. Let's compromise and call both viewpoints right. Durham seems to believe that God was incarnate in Trotsky; a sort of Church Militant Tendency.

I think your relativism is a kind of Buddhism, or perhaps

87

Christibuddhity. Its key word is unkowingly. I think you may have discovered agnosticism. But then why postulate 'the sort of God who produces the Universe?' Why not just *The Universe*? It's more economical, by an infinite margin. Then of course God can be immanent in it. The difficulty is that, according to most religionists, only the transcendence matters. But I quite agree with you: there's no virtue and no salvation, not to mention no sense, in seeking to understand what by definition we cannot. Let each seek God in what lies immediately to hand: in our friends, our lovers, our books and our garden. Let us address God as 'Your Immanence', indwelling in the topics and pursuits we find so curiously compulsive. Wherefore I perceive that there is nothing better, than that a man should rejoice in his own works, for that is his portion: for who shall bring him to see what shall be after him? Or of course *her* own works, e.g. on theology. Or, faute de mieux, Shakespeare's works.

Love as ever, E.

Otterbourne

August 21st, 22nd, 23rd, 24th, 1986

My dear E,

All I managed yesterday was to write your name and date and my address and I then worked myself into such a frenzy of frustration that nothing else transpired. I was expecting to turn a neat phrase of appreciation of your own amusing, welcome, news and views and then burst forthwith into a full-scale, full-blooded assessment of the concept of liberation theology. All in one go. But of course things don't happen like that. I remembered that after a good night's sleep. There is also a confession to be made. In mid-frustration I suddenly remembered the Test Match and turned on just in time to see Botham stride to his mark and take his epoch-making first ball wicket. Thereafter several hours were lost. I was *at* the Oval (where I made the 74 which got me on the Australian tour all those years ago) and it was helped I thought by good camera work showing players' expressions at interesting moments.

What will happen today? It's 9.40 a.m. so there is no

possibility of dereliction of duty for an hour and twenty minutes. Then I suspect the weather will take a hand. After a few early shafts of sunlight to brighten my half hour walk when I mean business, black clouds are gathering *en route* for Surrey and Middlesex.

One of the essays we were invited to submit last year was entitled "Liberation Theology — Theology or Politics?" and Alan Race has very kindly said he would not mind looking at anything I wrote after the end of term. This is jolly D, for an extra-mural mature student is a very lowly academic animal.

Liberation Theology — Theology or Politics?

Actually, we can plunge straight back into our discussion of six months ago when we had arrived at this precise point: viz., the coupling of atonement with salvation and liberation. See my letter of the end of February when I repeated — I could not help it — my deep distrust of the whole idea of salvation as an objective. And Alan Race (to whom these letters are duplicated) had provided a great shaft of illumination when he suggested that for the dreaded salvation, one might try speaking of liberation at many levels instead.

Still recapping, you write back smartly on February 28th, on Heisenberg's uncertainty principle and thoughts to do with physics, which however I propose to abandon for the time being until I feel stronger. On matters theological, however, we find ourselves for once in agreement. Neither of us can do with blood and sacrifice. And you too jib at salvation.

You write (irreverently some would say, but of course to you as an atheist one cannot be irreverent) — "How did God come to have this mad obsession with blood?" and I reply "Easy, my dear Watson. It is not God who has a mad obsession with blood but the early Israelites, those primitive tribesmen of our earlier letters, to whom religion without sacrifice was unthinkable — so that the early Christians were at one time held to be atheists because they worshipped *without* sacrifice" (See Frances Young, précised in my letter of February 21-4. p. 8). It all helps to confirm to me that the God against whom you inveigh, the Jehovah of the Old Testament, is not an objective reality at all but a highly culturally determined construct of these primitive tribesmen etc.

Second: jibbing at salvation you wondered "just what exactly it is that (you) and the rest of *femina/homo sapiens* have been guilty *of*, or atoned *for*, or redeemed *from*?" Well, I can think of many things, but primarily man's inhumanity to man, Auschwitz. The holocaust. (Incidentally, these events have cast a deep shadow over liberal theology, as one becomes aware. So much theological thinking originates in Germany, and evidently German theologians are shattered to an extent we can barely imagine.)

To go back to what it is that the human race is guilty of, the great point about modern sin, to coin a phrase, is that it extends beyond the personal to the societal and the planetary, the three levels at which liberation (salvation) may be effected, according to another telling marginal note by our tutor. Auschwitz, on this reading, involved sin both personal and societal: orders were orders. On the planetary level, see Romans 8: 20, where Paul linked groaning creation with Christ's liberating (saving) power. And back again to human society, it is precisely at another gross social ill, namely the oppression of the poor and the marginalised and the non-persons (their terminology) that liberation theology is directed.

So what *is* Liberation Theology? Here is the definition of Gustavo Gutierrez, the Peruvian priest who is the original principal academic apologist for the movement.

"The theology of Liberation is an attempt to understand the faith from within the concrete historical, liberating, and subversive praxis of the poor of this world — the exploited classes, despised ethnic groups and marginalised cultures. It is born of a disquieting unsettling hope of liberation (Gutierrez — *The power of the poor in history*, p. 37).

I have to confess that I am immediately turned off by another seminal word, *praxis*. At first hearing (just the other day) it sounded like Marxist invention, but the Concise Oxford Dictionary gives the derivation as mediaeval French and Latin, and Greek.[1] Can you, as a

90

professional word-monger, throw any light on it?

To show how liberation theology fits in, Gutierrez, who shines through as a devout son of the Church, gives an interesting historical review of theological preoccupations over the centuries (See *A theology of Liberation*). For almost the entire history of the church, two classical functions persist, he says; theology as wisdom, and theology as rational knowledge. So far as wisdom is concerned, theology in the early centuries was linked to the spiritual life. Meditation on the Bible was the road to spiritual growth and this was particularly so in the monastic life. Linked with platonism by the Greek fathers, it concentrated on metaphysics and undervalued the present life which it regarded as contingent. Theology regarded as rational knowledge began from the twelfth century onwards to establish itself as a science; and then, by St. Thomas Aquinas, as an intellectual discipline. After the thirteenth century, however, a degradation of the Thomist conception begins to appear, and after the Council of Trent theology became gradually *an ancillary discipline to the magisterium of the church* (my italics), whose function became "to define, present and explain revealed truths; to examine doctrine, to denounce and condemn false doctrines and to defend true ones; to teach revealed truths authoritatively."

Recent years have seen the development of two further theological functions: viz., stress has been laid on existential and active aspects of the Christian life, the faith being seen as a going-out of oneself, a commitment to God and neighbour, a relationship with others.

And also, crucially, comes the function of critical reflection on praxis, which is the place assigned to reflective theology in the liberation theology scheme of things. However, Gutierrez points out that this too had its roots in the early Church, in St. Augustine's *City of God*. (And to this the Anglican would add F.D. Maurice with his *Christian Socialism*, and William Temple, and others.) But it shows Gutierrez' passionate concern to proclaim that

91

liberation theology is biblically based and very much part of main-stream Christianity.[2]

As to how the rest of the theory goes I turn to my lecture notes supplemented by Gutierrez' *The Power of the Poor in History*. This is a collection of conference addresses written ten years after his seminal *Theology of Liberation*, which was out of print, out of the Lyttleton Library and generally inaccessible. So I had to buy *The Power of the Poor* which of its nature is less well constructed. Never mind.

The heart of the matter is the priority of (this wretched!) praxis[3] and the option for the poor. Praxis is for Gutierrez and his fellows the test of truth. For them it is action, practice, praxis, that counts rather than thought,[4] and it is thought rather than action that has dominated the classical European theological scene — (which is doubtless why the Vatican does not go overboard for L.T. — though the Pope himself may be a different matter). As Edward Shillebeeckx said in an interview "It is evident that thought is also necessary for action. But the Church has for centuries devoted her attention to formulating truths and meanwhile did almost nothing to better the world. In other words, the Church focussed on orthodoxy and left orthopraxis in the hands of non-members and non-believers."

But it is how one gets from[5] this priority of praxis, so-called, to the option for the poor, that foxes me. My notes proclaim that all theology has to be mediated and related to historical praxis: or in plain English, the Christ-event has to be mediated, or interpreted in the light of present circumstances.[6] That seems clear enough. This is what all courses based on liberal theology are about. But my notes go on to say that in order to understand the principle of mediation an analysis of social and political conditions is required, and that the tools of this analysis are Marxist and revolutionary. The roots of injustice are said to lie with the structure of capitalism which thrives on competition (thus setting up antagonistic forces between groups in society) and exploitation based on private ownership for profit.

92

Without a thoroughgoing analysis of this kind a system of social services and development prevails and easily absorbs the cause to right the wrongs of injustice into its own political outlook. The option for the poor remains ignored at root.

Thus sin is manifest in corporate life (as we said earlier). *What* is it, at root, at basic root, that makes the rich man in his castle, the poor man at his gate? Capitalism. The Marxist analysis of capital and exploitation provides a map of the structure of sin as this is manifest in corporate life . . . 'Original sin' now relates to society and not to biology and personal demeanor as it did with Augustine.

So this is the quantum leap, the epistemological break, and other dicta of this theology. The only means of leaping from the priority of praxis (which I can accept) to the priority of the poor[7] (which to me is less securely based) is via Marxist analysis which I definitely reject.

Ones suspicion is deepend when one turns to consider liberation theology in relation to christology and the Kingdom of God. The liberation theologian, steeped in praxis, turns to inspect the praxis of Jesus and discovers there that it too exemplified the option for the poor. For him the traditional tenets of christology, incarnation, resurrection, experience of the risen Lord, proclamation of the kerygma, count as nothing in comparison with the historical deeds of Jesus. And now I quote a few passages which I have underlined in Gutierrez *The power of the poor in history*, in which, interpret as you may, the passages are construed to bear more than the actual scriptures say, in my view . . .

"The nub, the nucleus, of the biblical message, we have said is in the relationship between God and the poor. Jesus Christ is precisely *God become poor*. This was the human life he took — a poor life. And this is the life in and by which we recognise him as Son of his Father." (p. 13.)

"Jesus' death is the consequence of his struggle for justice, his proclamation of the kingdom, *and his identification with the poor*." (p. 14.) (my italics)

and lastly

> "The celebration of the Lord's Supper presupposes a
> communion and solidarity with the poor in history.
> Without this solidarity, it is impossible to comprehend the
> death and resurrection of the Servant of Yahweh." (p. 16.)

It is these passages, in which 'the poor' are promoted to a
position of absolute pre-eminence to which I object.[8] (For, as you
and I would ask — where do the disabled, and all who suffer for
reasons other than exploitation figure in all this?) I hasten to
add that Gutierrez has some very perceptive things to say about
love and justice when we can leave the poor out of the reckoning
for one moment, viz.,

> "Knowledge of God is love of God. In the language of the
> Bible, 'to know' is not something purely intellectual. To
> know means to love." (p. 8.)

(I seem to remember hearing that the Hebrew word for
knowing means also loving in the sense of having sexual
intercourse. But that's *entirely* by the way!)

And quite simply,

> 'To know God is to do Justice.' (p. 7.)

There is one further important heading under which
liberation theology must be considered, that of revolution.
Gutierrez is well aware that he could stand accused of fostering
revolution but is too good a theologian to fall into that particular
trap. Christian liberation is not political liberation. The
kingdom is not to be identified with any particular revolution.

On the other hand, some social systems manifest the values of
the Kingdom more than others.

I have written enough. We shall all be tired out. But I have
still one or two comments to make, essentially personal, pro and
con.

Con first. One may re-read the gospels in an endeavour to
detect therein Jesus' exclusive emphasis on the poor which

94

Gutierrez finds.[9] Not me. Granted, there is the fact of Jesus' poor circumstances and background. Granted, there is the parable of Lazarus and the rich man with all his doomed brothers; and the widow's mite and above all, the other rich man who could not bring himself to sell all that he had to give to the poor, for he was very rich (Mark 10) which led to the reflection how hard it is for rich people to enter the Kingdon of God, harder than for a camel to go through the eye of a needle.

And this is another tricky little problem solved by the way. Did you know that "the eye of the needle" is a narrow little passage for foot-passengers in one of the main gates of Jerusalem — it could be the Damascus gate? Too narrow for a camel to get through. I learned this on our lightening Holy Land trip two years ago.

But to go back to the gospels: surely one is left with the certainty that the Gospel *has* to be for everyone.[10] I am.

Re-capping, reviewing, summarising, it seems to me that liberation theology falls short of a total Christian theology[11] — it bends too many rules. Which leaves it as a powerful political movement, and a worthy one at that, as all movements throughout history on behalf of liberty — freedom — liberation have been worthy. Oppression must be very oppressive to make a worm turn.

Does it have relevance in the West? Clearly it suits conditions in Southern and Central America, where from the Conquistadors onwards, exploitation has been the order of the day. And that is where it has taken root, as it may well take root in Africa and other third-world primary producers. But what about Western democracy and its values, shaped in the U.K. not only by Pitt and Burke but by Lord Shaftesbury, Methodism, the early Trade Unions and Labour movement (not so sure about later ditto), together with a host of comparatively minor influences? Surely, when our particular brand of democracy is working it ensures the absence of de-personalisation, and of marginalization? Do not the social security provisions ensure an absence of starvation?

The answer to these rhetorical questions is not the clear-cut affirmative one would hope for. I was shocked the other day to hear a woman say on the radio, "It's no good me ringing the Town Hall. No one takes any notice of an unemployed person on housing benefit." If that's not de-personalisation, marginalisation, what is?

Further, we in the rich West must find some way of re-distributing wealth in favour of the poor — that is the international, indeed planetary dimension of institutional sin for which means of restitution must be found. And closer at home, the problems of the inner cities remind all who have ears to hear that the price, not only of democracy, but of respecting the personalities of black neighbours, and of ensuring their participation in the economic, civic and democratic processes, also requires eternal vigilance. Eternal vigilance but not Marxist revolution.[12]

End August 1986

E.,

Another word about transcendence and immanence and your last letter. Let each indeed search for — and find God in his friends, his lovers, his books — (music?) and garden (not me this last). But that makes it too subjective even for me. I can spy graven images round every corner. There *has* to be something else, and this is what I believe is called the 'normative' aspect of Christ, i.e. the establishment of a value system which places his values first — love, self-sacrifice etc. (but *not* miracles other than the miracles of changes of heart). And surely this value system has to have an independent validity other than what occurs in friends and lovers — something recognisable as Other. How else do you identify it in immanence?

Do you understand what I am trying to say? I'm not sure I do myself!

All love till Friday,

Nancy

5 September 1986

Dear Nancy,

I'm really in no state to offer any comments on your sprightly pages: but I promised a few, so here goes.

1. I'm all for substituting 'liberation' for 'salvation': but doesn't that mean substituting something else (what?) in place of Christianity. And I still want to know what I'm being *liberated* from.

2. It won't do, for me at least, to say that it wasn't God but the Israelites who have this weird obesession with blood. It's just generally Israeli. Jesus has it too, in overflowing measure. No doubt it has something to do with the tribal rituals of nomadic herdsmen: their slaughtering laws are still in force. It's Jesus as well as Jehovah who finds religion unthinkable without slaughtering and sacrifice and the sacramental symbolism of blood-drinking and torment. The Blood of the Lamb is actually what it's all about. It's not to my taste.

3. I don't understand how we're supposed to have been redeemed by Christianity from *Auschwitz*. Wasn't it, on the contrary, Christianity that *brought Auschwitz about*? My Jewish friends find the Cross just as terrifying as the swastika.

The notion that we are all somehow sinners in need of redemption seems to me not only obvious nonsense but the opposite of what Jesus actually said (admittedly from memory, on my way back from a solitary journey to and from my seaside homeland) "I come not to call the righteous but sinners to repentance". The prayer 'deliver us from evil' is surely not a request to be delivered from our own natures? Evil is an external force, throughout the New Testament, personified by Satan, in whose personal incarnation Jesus manifestly believes. It would never have occurred to Jesus, would it, that humankind was inherently wicked? If it is, and if Jesus was truly human, why wasn't Jesus wicked?

4. Liberation theology seems to me to have its own share of asserting the opposite of what Jesus said, namely "the poor you have with you always". That seems sensible enough. The reason isn't capitalism, or communism (where things are much the same): the reason is the inherent inequality of genetic endowment for which humanity as such is certainly not to blame. It's really very perverse of God to blame us for the readily forseeable results of his own decrees.

5. I think a very useful exercise would be simply to write down

what Jesus's system of values actually was, both as explicit in his own recorded words and actions and as inferable therefrom. I think anyone who dispassionately undertook such an exercise and objectively recorded its results would certainly bring close a revolution in theology. Liberation, in fact!

Sorry to be so negative and restricted. I'll try to do better after publication day.

Love as ever, E.

Otterbourne

September 18, 1986

My dear E,

Many thanks for your letter of September 5th which, owing to my Mediterranean spree, only hit me on the 15th and, as always, requires more than instant sunshine in reply. But I'm so sorry you are feeling depressed and dentisted; two very debilitating conditions.

Liberation: If you make a direct substitution for the dreaded salvation, you get liberated from sin, as you very well know. As to what sin is, it's personal sins of omission as well as commission e.g. just sitting there and not doing a thing about anybody beyond ones own family and friends — an attitude against which Jesus specifically warned us. (Luke 14: 7.) It's also — cf Alan Race, sin which can perpetrate Auschwitz — because so many Christians are less than Christians in action, particularly, to agree with you, in their relationship with the Jews (who have recently been officially cleared by the Pope of being responsible for the death of Jesus). Auschwitz = societal sin. As to Cross and Swastika, the latter is a mutilation of the former. And sin can be also global exploitation.

But of course it's impossible to be precise about sin, it seems to me, because Christianity is a religion of spirit and not of negative precept. So sin becomes any thought or action or relationship which does not square up with Christ's value-system interpreted as best one can with or without the authority of mother church according to the confession one belongs to.[13]

Obsession with blood: Yes — I'm with you here that all Jews,

98

and Jesus himself as a Jew, were and are brought up with the sacramental symbolism of animal sacrifice. But we are also told specifically that this is not what God requires — but a broken and contrite heart etc. And it was precisely because the early Christians broke with the animal sacrifice tradition and did *not* go in for ritual slaughter, that they were regarded by the contemporaries as atheists: *that's* the point.[14] Symbolism lingers on in Blood of the Lamb metaphor, granted. But it's only metaphor. The sacrifice demanded of Christians has for many hundreds of years consisted of time, money and self: not blood, surely.

Satan as an external force: another tricky one. My father believed in a devil. I don't. First century Jews, of whom Jesus was one, manifestly did. Modern historical Biblical scholarship takes all this in its stride, and writes off[15] many of Jesus' beliefs, and those of his contemporaries, as consistent with the historical period in which he lived, but not necessarily with today's knowledge. Look what happened to the Catholic Church when it became too specific in astronomy and physics: Galileo.

But when Jesus said he was calling sinners, not righteous, to repentance, I always took it that he said this tongue in cheek, knowing full well that the righteous were the biggest sinners of the lot.[16] How differently we sometimes see things — but with underlying agreement, I still hope.

The poor: for whom Liberation theology declares an option. I followed a suggestion you made when we discussed the subject, and combed through the gospels to remind myself precisely what Jesus had said about them. I did it as holiday homework, in a deckchair on the Palmers' terrace.

Two and a half pages of foolscap boil down to this. On the rich/poor question Jesus's chief pre-occupation is to warn against the accummulation of riches because wherever our treasure is, there will our heart be also and we cannot serve God and mammon (money). I won't labour the point because we are all so familiar with these passages.

Correspondingly, Jesus calls the poor fortunate for they shall inherit the earth and enter the kingdom. The good news is preached to them (Luke 4: 16) (and also to the captive and the blind), but of a heavenly, not an earthly kingdom.[17] There is no suggestion that they are to become rich too.

Without actually counting words, it seems to me that more, or at any rate just as much, is said by Jesus about the powerful and the powerless, the first and the last, also about eating with tax collectors and outcasts, and being the slave of all. Look up the argument among the disciples about who is to be the greatest and sit at the Lord's right hand; and, the washing of the disciples' feet. I wonder if 'powerless' is a permissible translation of the Greek usually rendered as 'humble'? I wonder if it is the same as liberation theology's 'marginalised' and 'non-persons'? One rather suspects so.[18] And I can think of few more 'marginalised' people than former psychiatric patients discharged into an unwaiting world. This is where, probably because of previous concerns, I personally view the great relevance of Liberation theology to our own society. But it obviously applies to the grossly disadvantaged of every sort, including ethnic minorities (but not all) physically disabled, and so on.[19]

I'm going to whizz this off to you in advance of something on Christ's finality and religious pluralism, which may well be quite long, not only because it's Alan Race's special subject but because it encapsulates the main twentieth century debate on the Incarnation and I cannot and must not hurry it.

It will incidentally be helped by another of your suggestions, viz — to write down what Jesus' system of values actually was. This is twentieth century language, understood by all. I will try and do that too, but it certainly won't bring about a revolution in today's liberal theology: I don't think so.

Nancy

Otterbourne

September 21st
various to October 6

My dear E,

Here comes the sequel, the promised discussion on what the

claim to Christ's finality can mean in relation to other religious traditions. It's a very up-to-date discussion, I find, sharpened by the consequences of a shrinking world and also by the extraordinary *volte-face* of the Catholic Church after the Second Vatican Council, whereby so many things now become possible which previously were not so. It is typified by an anecdote heard the other day on the radio — about the disposal of a redundant Anglican church for some proper purpose, and the powers that were (I forget who) opted for a devout Sikh group rather than a curious so-called Christian sect.

Briefly, is Jesus' saying (John 14: 6) "I am the way, and the truth and the life: no one comes to the Father, but by me," to be taken quite literally, 'as Gospel truth', or isn't it?

Considering the matter, one can anchor oneself by a couple of catch-phrases which have come to epitomise the polarity of the positions taken up. You get *the scandal of particularity* if you stick to the rigorist view of the incarnation which has characterised most of church history for two thousand years. By which it is meant that Christ is indeed the only way and therefore all the other religious traditions just simply don't count in God's purposes. In previous letters you have protested at the ridiculous prospect this results in, the billions of years of pre-history, and the millions of people in heathen lands afar who have simply not had the opportunity, for reasons of time and space of being introduced to Christ's gospel. Others feel the same way, and also point to the relative lack of success of missionary endeavour when this comes up against the major other religious traditions, Judaism, Islam, Hinduism, Buddhism, Taoism. (Incidentally, I am very hampered by my ignorance of these religions to any depth, though I remember to this day a fierce discussion on re-incarnation with the *dewan*, prime minister, of the tiny central Indian state where my father worked — and played — as a young man. So I can only talk in general terms.) Where Christian missions have flourished, it is pointed out, is where they supplanted primitive animist beliefs. One is confronted therefore with the really very tricky question: can the almost wholesale rejection, by the sophisticated other faiths, of the Christian gospel, really be the last word in this debate?

But I have once again jumped the gun. It is worth looking at

101

the formidable array of opinion, from towering theologians such as Karl Barth, to everyday mid-West born-again Americans, who stick to, and indeed vigorously propogate, the rigorist view. Not forgetting of course, the whole *magisterium* of the Catholic church until Vatican II. Strange bed-fellows.

Karl Barth (1886-1968) was a name to conjure with among S.C.M. members in the Oxford of the 30s: though I had little idea what he stood for. This is very sympathetically outlined in his *No other name?* (S.C.M. Press 1985) by Paul Knitter whose stance, as a sort of Roman Catholic pluralist, is diametrically opposed to his.

First, Karl Barth agrees (for once) with liberal theologians that we cannot know God: therefore we cannot find him by ourselves: we must recognise the infinitely qualitative distinction, the impenetrable distinction, between God and man.[20]

From this it follows that only God himself can show us God. Which he does through the Incarnation, the sole point of revelation. All other forms of religion, including versions of the Christian religion other than his own, are stigmatized as unbelief "Religion is Unbelief" is the catch-phrase here, an extraordinary and paradoxical statement taken in isolation without the run-up given above.

It goes without saying that all non-Christian religions don't stand a chance, with him. But is also carries a further devastating sequel (*Christians and Religious Pluralism*. Alan Race. S.C.M. Press 1983)

> "Any attempt on the part of man to anticipate, predict, or supply criteria out of his own reason by which the gospel may be interpreted, is a direct contradiction of the meaning and the act of revelation" (p. 12)

So much for liberal theology! And two of Barth's followers Kraemer and Brunner also insist on the absoluteness of Christ's fulfillment of all religion and the judgment on all religion. (Brunner. *Revelation and Religion* 1947 p. 270.)

The trouble is: the whole system is water-tight, *a priori*, inaccessible. But it does not stop the Fundamentalists and

Evangelicals from embracing it whole-heartedly, to such effect that, according to a Gallup poll, 30% of Americans are evangelicals. And they are supported by a vast international network, who, meeting in 1974 at Lausanne as the International Congress on World Evangelization, could deliver themselves of the following.

"We also reject as derogatory to Christ and the Gospel every kind of syncretism and dialogue which implies that Christ speaks equally through all religions and theologies. Jesus Christ, being himself the only God-man, who gave himself as the only ranson for sinners, is the only mediator between God and man. There is no other name by which we must be saved. All men are perishing because of sin, but God loves all men, not wishing that any should perish – but that all should repent. Yet those who reject Christ repudiate the joy of salvation and condemn themselves to eternal separation from God. To proclaim Jesus as "the saviour of the world" is not to affirm that all religions offer salvation in Christ. Rather it is to proclaim God's love for a world of sinners and to invite all men to respond to him as Saviour and Lord in the whole-hearted personal commitment of repentance and faith. Jesus Christ has been exalted above every other name. We long for the day when every knee shall bow to him and every tongue shall call him Lord."
(From the Lausanne Covenant)

And so we come to the other main strand in exclusivist belief — the Roman Catholic church before Vatican II, the position of which was characterised by the dictum "Outside the Church, no salvation". This position was first formulated by Origen (d. 254) and Cyprian (d. 258), but it is a relief to know that its starkness was from the earliest centuries counterbalanced by an attitude not far removed from Karl Rahner's anonymous Christianity — see later section. None the less in its heyday, shaped by barbarian invasion and Augustinian doctrine which united to save the church in its worldly form as well as its heavenly, the Church could go so far as to assert that to belong properly one had to accept papal authority too. All of which is meat and drink to the liberal historian who can without difficulty tease out the reasons for such a retreat behind the stockades. (Knitter p. 121.) Not that this attitude and belief is entirely a thing of the past among Roman Catholics. Apparently there are many who view the loosening process of Vatican II with something like dismay. I met one the other day in Malvern, when I was collecting my Liverpool Irish fast bowler friend Mac. from her mass.

I mentioned useful catch-phrases. *"Debilitating Relativism"* is what you get, say some, if you adopt the opposite to the exclusivist position, namely pluralism. This is what you get, say these critics, if you abstract Christs' finality and uniqueness and fudge the issue. For pluralism means that Christ's finality can be defined in such a way as to co-exist with other religions on an equal footing. And if all religions are on the same footing, what is there to live and die for: that is specifically Christian?

Ernst Troeltsch (1865-1923), philosopher, theologian and once regarded as a potential candidate for the presidency of the Weimer Republic, in one of the big names here, his successive viewpoints transparently and rather endearingly plotted in his successive writings.

Troeltsch spent his life battling with the reconciliation of the two opposing viewpoints noted above — exclusivism and relativism. On the one hand (relativism) there was historical consciousness: human beings were not only rational and social beings but historical beings. We live in historical cultures and all movements of the human spirit are conditioned in historical circumstances. This includes religion: so that religion and its interpretation change through time. All is limited and relative, and this applies also to the Kantian filter of human understanding. No amount of yearning will bring the absolute within reach. No historical manifestation of the absolute can be absolute. Thus there can be no absolute religion, for no religion can claim that it stands above this all-embracing (absolute!) relativity.

Having arrived at this position, Troeltsch had enormous difficulty including his belief in the superiority of Christianity, which he also held. I have been poring over pages in Knitter to try and hoist this reconciliation on board, and have to admit that I don't get it![21]

On to another major figure, still very much alive and now located in California, whither he transferred himself from a chair at Birmingham University — John Hick. I read an early book of his on the philosophy of religion (brilliant) and he was of course, a contributor to the *Myth of God Incarnate*. He shares with Troeltsch the characteristic of plotting his successive emotional, intellectual (? spiritual) positions: and when major thinkers do this, it does get very confusing. However, here all that one needs to comprehend is that if one considers the incarnation to be a myth — (to which he would add — none the worse for that) — the accommodation of alternative religions becomes child's play. And of course I'm over-simplifying all the time, which can't be helped in the span of a letter.[22]

But, re-reading the above after a lapse of several days, I realise that John Hick deserves better than such cavalier dismissal — his myth-making is positive rather than iconoclastic. In particular he has stitched together an ingenious and pretty logical pluralist scheme which he calls his *Copernican Revolution*. As the sun replaced the earth as the centre of the planetary universe so God replaced Christ and Christianity as the centre of the religious universe. God was at the centre of a range of manners of knowing culturally and geographically determined — viz — the different religions. And the adherents to the different religions, through varieties of religious experience thus encounter the one ultimate divine reality. The trouble about Hick, for many people including me, is that this reality is not the revealed God of the Christian incarnation. And a second great problem is that if *all* religions are equally valid as in this scheme, what criteria remain for assessing their relative values? Or don't they have valid differences of value? Of course they do, says she crossly! Who wants to be an Islamic fundamentalist, chopping off peoples' hands?

To recap: The finality of Christ and pluralism cannot co-exist. My own position, I realise, is that labelled by Alan Race *inclusivist*, and reported by him as being probably the majority position among theologians today. The extraordinary thing is that it came from a Roman Catholic stable via the great Karl Rahner; and when I look back to the days of my youth, and the heated and unedifying arguments held with the only sorts of Roman Catholics then permitted, namely the fiercely exclusivist of earlier pages, I marvel indeed.

What *is* the inclusivist position? Race defines it as aiming "to hold together two equally binding convictions; the operation of the grace of God in all the great religions of the world working for salvation, and the uniqueness of the manifestation of the grace of God in Christ, which makes a universal claim on the final way of salvation" (*Christians and religious pluralism*. Race p.38). It is also a position with very respectable, *very* early antecedents, viz. S. Paul on Aeropagus identifying the unknown God as the Christian God, and Justin Martyr, writing probably much about the same time as Luke, proclaiming in accordance with logos-type thinking

> "Christ is the divine word in whom the whole human race share, and those who live according to the light of their knowledge are Christians even if they are considered as being Godless."
>
> (Apology 46 1-4)

— shades already of Karl Rahner's famous *anonymous Christianity*, and indeed it was apparently Rahner above all who was responsible for the new Vatican look, the post-conciliar look. I hope you won't get fed up with too many quotes, but I really do believe that this still quite recent, still not universally adopted official Roman Catholic position is so important that the greatest emphasis should be laid upon it. So I quote again, the *locus classicus*, from the Papal encyclical *Nostra Aetate*.

> "The Catholic Church rejects nothing of what is true and holy in these religions. She has a high regard for the manner of life and conduct, the precepts and doctrines, which although differing in many ways from her own teaching, nevertheless often reflect a ray of that truth which enlightens all men"

It goes on, however —

> . . . "Yet she proclaims and is in duty bound to proclaim without fail Christ who is the way, the truth and the life (John 14: 6). In him, in whom God reconciled all things to

himself (2 Cor. 5: 18), men find the fulness of their religious life."

The anonymous Christianity part comes into the picture because according to Rahner, only Christianity presumes to name the reality which is anonymously present in other faiths including in their rites and ceremonies. Others have followed him, including Hans Küng (frowned on by the Vatican — why?) and our own John Robinson. I find myself in substantial *rapport* with Hans Küng, I think, because he believes Christ to be, not so much the *author* or salvation in other faiths (which is such an abstract concept as to be almost unintelligible) — as *normative*. That is to say, Christ is "ultimately decisive, definitive, archetypal for man's relations with God."

I find myself wholeheartedly going along with the fraternal sentiments expressed in *Nostra Aetate*, but at the end of the day it seems to me one *has* to retain Christ as defining the difference between good and evil, no matter what the content of other religions may be. I can't go along with Alan Race when he stigmatises this position as 'unjustified theological imperialism.' [23]

30 October 1986

Dear Nancy,

No sooner had I read through your latest ebullient bulletin (September 21-October 6) than the Second Vatican Council came at me from another direction — via the latest (rather pallid) biography of G.K. Chesterton. How could he or Belloc have endured that vole-face? It would have annihilated all they ever stood for or believed in. Becoming a Catholic now is utterly different from being one then. Still, I don't see why God wouldn't change direction from time to time, or aeon to aeon: just to see whether we're attending. Yet on the actual question did Jesus mean what he is said to have said (John 14: 6) I'm sure that I am the way has no two ways about it. How can we take those words at their volte face value? It seems to me that *The scandal of particularity* is just what used to be called Christianity.

The argument you attribute to Karl Barth strikes me as

107

exceedingly singular. I shall strive to set it down again step by step to further my understanding. It begins (1) we cannot know God: (2) we need help in finding him: so (3) he has provided the Incarnation etc.

But surely this is an argument which not only fails to follow from its premises but *actively contradicts* them? A procedure not normally reckoned all that syllogistic. How in the world or out of it can we deduce or infer that *any agency whatever* can show us God, from the datum that *no agency whatever can* do so?

I rather like, though, the dictum that any attempt on our part to interpret the gospel via reason is a direct contradiction of revelation. What that proves, though, is that revelation is *irrational*, which I've long suspected. Come to think of it, though, it would have to be, wouldn't it, if it is ever to convey anything significant to the human mind, which is utterly rebarbative to reason (as I know from my Shakespeare studies).

In my present euphoric mood I should like to offer a modest solution to this whole cosmic problem. It's this: enquiring minds act as receivers, open to (in this analogy) reflected sky-wave.

What signals we pick up depends on our sensitivity, posture, location and so forth. We know by observation that there's a variety and span of different transmitters. Now, it seems to me arrogantly reductionist to assert, in such circumstances, that Jesus is *only one* broadcasting station among others (albeit the one with the best News). We really rather *know* that on that analogy he's inaudible in many areas. So when he said I am the way, meaning surely that here is only one, he *couldn't* have meant there's only one *transmitter*, callsign JC, on X kiloherz, because everyone can see there's more than one. He must have meant there's only one signal: and that's him, in various guises. Could we ask Alan Race whether he's really offering to restrict The Almighty to just *one* revelation? That would be Raceism with a vengence. No doubt *I am the way* etc. must mean that there's *only one* something or other, the question is what is there only one of? Art may be a surer guide than religion: there are no aesthetic, only doctrinal, problems about uniting in diversity. If Mozart had said that he was the way to music I'd have understood him perfectly: it means that which is Mozartian, i.e.

marvellous. Schubert has it too, only we then call it Schubertian. So many ways: yet all in the same direction: hence One Big Broad Bright and probably Milky Way.

Well perhaps I should try again, with another brandy from the buffet, but pragmatically I'd want to ask — since there *must be* some means of reconciling the apparent contradiction between 'I am the only way/there are, however others' perhaps it doesn't matter all that much what the answer is. I think that Troeltsch is wasting his time in striving and searching for a formal reconciliation between Exclusivism and Relativism. Why can't those two opposites just learn to love one another?

I agree with you that the correct interpretation is a mythinterpretation. Hick opus, Hick labor est.

And I'd like to put in a plea for the inclusion of artistic experience amony the possibilities or potentials.

I very much liked, incidentally, the decision to award the redundant Anglican church premises to those paragons of turban civilisation the Sikhs. Sikh and ye shall find, I expect they said.

Love, as ever, E

Otterbourne

December 2, 3, 4, 1986

My dear E,

Here we come to the last of the essay-type letters I shall be sending you based on the syllabus and experience of last session's course on Doctrine. The very fact that our tutor chose to deliver his final lecture on feminist theology rather than say, the sacraments, which of course also figure in the syllabus, illustrates an important point. We plunge straight into the midst of contemporary issues: not merely fashionable but issues furiously exercising the mind of the church today. By contrast, the sacraments are not currently a matter of contention. Indeed, the Anglican-Roman Catholic commision on doctrine, ARCIC, has arrived at a joint understanding on the nature of the eucharist which would have been unthinkable a few short years ago. So I understand.

So here I am, trying to assess the claim that Christian theology has been male-biased and therefore oppressive to women. I think that once again, I had better jump straight in and proclaim the standpoint from which I see things. After all it's my essay.

The male bias, for there has been male bias and it has been oppressive to women, springs (once again) straight from the Old Testament,[24] which (to my mind and as I have emphasised frequently these last two years) obstinately occupies a still too prominent position in Christian thinking. It springs, pre-eminently, straight from the Ten Commandments. "Thou shalt not covet thy neighbour's house; thou shalt not covet thy neighbour's wife, nor his manservant, nor his maidservant, nor his ox, nor his ass, nor anything that is his." A woman is a possession, like other possessions, in a divinely ordained hierarchical society.

The new covenant of Jesus by contrast comes on a completely new wavelength.[25] The emphasis is on love, service and sacrifice, all of which have to be given voluntarily as children of God, as friends not as slaves. But women cannot partake of this new kingdom whose components are love and service unless *they have the freedom to offer love and service.* You cannot give under constraint. This is my simple, and to my mind, incontrovertible thesis.

Feminist theologians, however, tracing the history of male bias go back beyond Moses and the ten commandments, right back to the myths of the creation and paradise lost: back to the portrayal of womankind formed from the rib of man, to woman as original sinner, tempted and temptress. To woman physically second-class and morally defective.

And here I cannot do better than quote from a notable American theologian, Rosemary Ruether. Alas the title of her major feminist work turns one right off, "*Sexism and God-Talk*" is almost more than I can take, but after all, it isn't the title that matters. The book itself is *well* worth reading — a host of fresh insights for us stick-in-the-muds over here.

110

Though I note that these two books stem from endowed lectures not only in the States but in Holland. After which, I propose to quote not from "*Sexism and God-talk*" but "*To Change the World*", SCM, 1981.

"Christology", she writes (page 45) "has been the doctrine of the Christian tradition that has been most frequently used against women. Historically this anti-woman use of Christology reached its clearest formulation in the high scholasticism of Thomas Aquinas. Aquinas argued that the male is the formative or generic sex of the human species. Only the male represents the fulness of human potential, whereas woman by nature is defective physically, morally and mentally. Not merely after the Fall, but in the original nature of things, woman's 'defective nature' confined her to a subserviant position in the social order. She is by nature under subjugation. Therefore it follows that the Incarnation of the Logos of God into the male is not a historical accident, but an ontological necessity. The male represents wholeness of human nature, both in himself and as head of the woman. He is the fulness of the image of God, whereas woman by herself does not represent the image of God and does not possess wholeness of humanity (Aquinas. *Summa Theologica*). This view of the male genesis character of the *imago dei* is also found in St. Augustine (*De Trinitate*).

"It follows for Aquinas that women cannot represent headship either in society or in the church. Her inability to be ordained followed from her defective or (as Aquinas put it, following Aristotle's biology) her 'misbegotten' nature. Just as Christ had to be incarnated in the male, so only the male can represent Christ. Mary Daly's succinct judgment in her book *Beyond God the Father* would seem to be fully vindicated in Aquinas' theology: 'When God is male, the male is God' " (p. 19).

The above represents the fundamental theological male bias, viz. that women are in the pre-ordained scheme of things inherently inferior.

There are also other charges of male bias, arguments

111

assembled in opposition to the idea of ordaining women and therefore virtually the same thing, which are so well-known now in view of the proceedings in the General Synod, as barely to need recapitulation: For instance, that Jesus's selection of twelve male disciples represented a calculated decision to exclude women. That in St. Paul's view, women do not stand in direct relation to God, but are connected to him only secondarily through the male. This comes in 1 Corinthians Chapter 2:

> "I want you to understand that Christ is supreme over every man, the husband is supreme over his wife, and God is supreme over Christ (v. 3).
> . . .
> "For a man has no need to cover his head, because he reflects the image and glory of God. But woman reflects the glory of man."

This is all tied up with women covering their heads in church, which was once the norm in Anglican churches as it still is in many Roman Catholic countries. But no Anglican makes an issue of this nowadays. So what on earth can be the validity of the principle of male superiority in this particular scriptural passage, all inextricably interwovan with this essentially culturally influenced head covering prescription? Needless to say, the argument about the selection of the twelve, when also viewed in the historical perspective of first century culture, looks by no means watertight either. Can you imagine two or three women hiking over the hills with the other disciples, in first century Palestine? The Catholic argument that the 2,000 year tradition of male priesthood ought to remain (? forever) intact may similarly be challenged by an appeal to drastically changed social circumstances. In any event, Catholic opposition to the ordination of women may not be so monolithic as we sometimes suppose,[26] despite the apparently quite explicit (and extremely friendly) exchange of letters between Pope John Paul II, the Archbishop of Canterbury and Cardinal Willebrands (Times July 1, 1986). I was astounded, when reading a book by the respected Catholic Johannine scholar Raymond E. Brown, to come across an appendix on the roles of women in the fourth

112

gospel openly contemplating the possibility of ordaining them to the priesthood. (*The Community of the Beloved Disciple*, Geoffrey Chapman 1979. p. 183.)

A quite different attitude towards women at first sight strikes one as the very reverse of oppressive, namely romanticising them, putting them on a romantic pedestal simply by virtue of their sex. Perhaps to use the word 'oppressive' here may be a bit strong, but surely, to cast any living soul into an *a priori* mould, solely on account of his or her physical attributes, is oppressive in a subtle way. You see it in the field of disablement: "Does he take sugar?" A person is viewed as a member of the category of "the disabled" (and also *accordingly* dotty?) rather than as a living, breathing, actual person with a disability.

In theology, where we now are, surely the supreme example is the treatment accorded to the Virgin Mary. In search of recognition of the female principle, rather dormant since the male *logos* got the upper hand of the female *sophia* or wisdom, the Christian tradition gradually elevated Mary to the most lofty pedestal imaginable. The resultant Mariolatry, which both exalts Mary's sex and yet denies its natural (or supernatural) fulfilment as sinful, has led to some curious and quite non-scriptural additions to Catholic doctrine — namely Mary's immaculate conception and assumption, both devised to overcome the 'taint' of actual carnal reproduction or any hint of sexuality. Surely, too, all the Bride of Christ imagery for the Church and for nuns, represents the symbolism of men obesessed with sex, albeit sublimated: it is all so unnatural. No wonder women find it so distasteful to be caste for ever in the role of sinners and temptresses simply because they are women.

Mariolatry has also, I suggest, helped to give rise to an obsession with motherhood. This is alive and well (see Margaret Hood. Times Jan. 18, 1986).

"Now what I have called mothering is not only her gift to her child but also her unique relationship with creation and with God. Since the Incarnation, this mothering, which binds women so inextricably to creation, has been given a new significance and meaning. It has at the same time bound her more deeply to creation but also elevated her

113

above it."

Well! But where I do agree with Mary Hood is in according the importance to women to offer fully and freely their specific feminine contributions (more of this later). Simply I disagree with her as to what these are. Why should it be motherhood, any more than the supreme contribution of the male sex is fatherhood? To think in these terms is to isolate, and concentrate excessively upon (once more) physical attributes. Tenderness, intuitive faculty may be, possibly an instinct of hospitality, and all the maternal-type characteristics. Yes, remembering that maternal instinct is implanted throughout the animal kingdom too. But others possess these qualities besides mothers.

A final observation while we are on this side of the rails, so to speak: on celibacy. I would feel happier about this, both for men and women, if celibacy were regarded solely as offering conditions in which celibates could place themselves ureservedly at the service of God and man. Husbands or wives and children must get in the way so. But I fear that a still present consideration is that sex is in itself viewed as sinful, and sexual activity as inimical to the highest calling of discipleship. *Pace* St. Paul, this seems particularly strange in view of the fact that St. Peter, the very rock on which the church was built, was himself married. (Matthew 8: 14, also Mark 1:30 and Luke 4:38.)

So far we have dealt with the pro side of the proposition, viz., arguing that Christian theology, male biased, has in fact been oppressive to women. Reading through my paragraphs, I am surprised at my own vehemence. I didn't know I had it in me. It must be very deep-seated. And it is perhaps all the more surprising because I shall now contend, with I hope equal strength, that women should not be ordained in this country at this very moment.

First, though, a word as promised on page 5 as to why (it seems to me) to deny ordination to women on principle would count as the ultimate oppression in the Christian life. Granted: such a denial would have the effect of denigrating essentially feminine qualities (which I contend do exist) and it might also confer by implication a seal of approval on the position of women in for example Islamic countries, not to mention cultural

114

backwaters much closer home, where their domination is total. But my main contention, gut feeling if you like, is that women in common humanity must be free equally with men to pursue existential encounter with God through Christ, as with fellow human beings. Equally free, that is, to answer the promptings of the Holy Spirit — for what differentiates a male from a female vocation? Free to pursue this vocation to the ultimate, which in our tradition leads to the celebration of the eucharist.[27]

So now I am free to argue that Christian theology has not been oppresive to women so long as it has been genuinely inspired by Christ, and not by the authoritarian, patriachal ethos of the Old Testament (which can on occasion include also St. Paul).[28] Feminist theologians have combed the Bible for passages to establish the enduring presence of the female principle, however overlaid this may have been most of the time. Mainly N.T. of course but not forgetting The Song of Songs (however did that get in?), in which each sex celebrates in such incomparable poetry the beauty of his and her beloved. I shall concentrate on Jesus' relationship with two women. First, the Samaritan at the well (John 4: 1-28, 39-41), with whom Jesus held a long friendly, ultimately life-shattering conversation of a sort not usual in first century Palestine —

> "At the moment Jesus' disciples returned, and they were greatly surprised to find him talking with a woman. But none of them said to her 'What do you want?' or asked him 'Why are you talking to her?' " (John 4: 27.)

After discussing life-saving water, the crunch of what nowadays might well be called an existential encounter comes when Jesus perceives her sexual past, which she promptly acknowledges, to elicit his rewarding words "You have told me the truth". (This is obviously the main point of the story — but I cannot forbear to mention the sequel in verses 39-41.) Many Samaritans believed in Jesus because the woman told them that he had told her everything she had ever done.

> "Many more believed because of his message, and they said to the woman 'We believe now, *not because of what you said,* but because we ourselves have heard him . . .' "

Plus ça change!)

The other woman, and no prizes for guessing right, of course has to be Mary, sister of Martha and Lazarus. The exquisite glimpses of her devotion to Jesus, sitting at his feet rather than helping Martha with the work: breaking the jar of precious perfume wherewith to anoint him (and for the moment, bother the poor and the bystanding grumblers) bear in our present context what I should have thought was an unmistakeable meaning. Spelt out, it is that women should not be tied to household jobs when, so to speak, the King of Glory passes by: nor should they be ticked off for openhanded generosity, breaking the jar of precious perfume and so on, in the same circumstances. And, again, bother the insensitive (male) bystanders: nay, disciples. Does not this story, yet again, betoken the existential encounter par excellence? And if this Mary is Mary Magdalene (I have suddenly realised that I don't know — does anybody?)[29] — then the resurrection appearances too exemplify first-hand, unmediated encounter.

Now, may I jump straight to the present day. To believe in the eventual ordination of women does not confer approval of raucous feminist tactics for bringing this about. Access to higher education, equal pay in teaching, the professions, the civil service and so on, provide the platform, illustrate the progress of women's emancipation which alone make it possible to consider the times as being historically appropriate. But priesthood is not a job like any other: my previous pages bulge with ideas as to what it is rather than this, specifically to elevate the feminine contribution to the highest level in the church, so that the whole of humanity is represented. In the arguments about male and female knowing, role differentiation and so on, I find myself firmly on the side of the differentiators. But not so all my fellow-students. At our last lecture I screwed myself up to speak as follows:

"Value judgments are seldom made these days. But my value judgment is: Maleness is good: Femaleness is good. Therefore you have to have complementarity and sexual stereotyping has theologically absolutely nothing to do with it. Vive la différence!" [30]

116

This little speech was greeted with astonishment and stony silence.

It follows, from this view of complementarity, that women's eventual contribution to the priestly role will be uniquely feminine and none the worse for that.[31] It will also follow, as I see it, that they need not be completely interchangeable with men in specific posts.[32]

As I look round, I don't see that these and other insights of much more learned and important people than me, have sunk in enough to make this development — as a matter of sheer practical politics — a wise step. Catholic opposition, the opposition of all high Christologists, may not be so total as one supposes. But within the Anglican church itself, a bit of water should surely flow under the bridges. To take premature action in an atmosphere of threats of schism cannot be progressive.

Perhaps it all boils down, now that the theological case is so largely accepted, to this matter of the wise implementation of change. As you know, I have been cutting the *Times* and have several box files of cuttings. None more succinct and thoughtful than an article by Alan Webster, Dean of St. Paul's, on managing obedience to change (Times. July 5, 1986).

"Paul, the Apostle of the gentiles, saw that the Church was faced by great challenges: the divisions between Jews and gentiles, between slaves and freemen, between men and women. The first was dealt with by the first generation of Christians. The second had to wait for William Wilberforce and the third is now facing the churches of our day . . . In successive centuries, Christians have found it hard to manage change."

. . . Carrying one's cross does not mean only the trials which face everyone, but making the changes required by the obedience to God."

Must get this off to you. Look forward to lunch at the Club on Tuesday 9th, and I hope this gets to you before that.

Love as ever, Nancy.

117

YEAR II

NOTES

By Alan Race, Tutor, Doctrine Course.

1. p. 90 The word *praxis* is indeed cental in Marxist thought, and probably not used in Christian writing before Marx.

2. p. 92 He (Gutierrez) would probably say it was what mainstream Christianity lost.

3. p. 92 *'Praxis'* at its simplest is practice.

4. p. 92 It is not that thought does not count, it is that thought is secondary "a second act".

5. p. 92 'How one gets from.' What do you want to get from to? Theology? Liberation theologians say that has no value of its own.'

6. p. 92 'Present circumstances.' Not just 'present circumstances' like that. But a commitment to political and economic change.

7. p. 93 Liberation theology *begins* with a commitment to change on behalf of the poor. There is no need to argue from priority of praxis *to* priority of poor. One's praxis is *with* the poor, in order to change structural as well as individual priorities.

8. p. 94 The poor is a collective term to include all who suffer at the hands of oppressive structures and divisive policies of political and economic laws. People do suffer for all kinds of reasons often not having to do with poverty etc. Liberation theology does not deal directly with this. Perhaps we could say the *priority* of the Gospel is towards (through their eyes) the exploited poor etc. Liberation theologians do not idolise or idealise the poor for their own sake; it's not a virtue to be poor. It is that commitment to change will be different if you are poor than if you are rich. The rich, without giving up their power, will only ever be condescending. The pre-eminence of the poor is perhaps their question: "What is the Gospel for me?" Which Gospel promotes justice, and which keeps things the way they always have been?"

The poor are not chosen because they suffer, but because of the injustice.

9. p. 95 Jesus was concerned to announce the Kingdom. That will be received differently by the poor and the rich. The Kingdom includes justice etc. and it is the poor (for Gutierrez *et al*) who know what justice means when it occurs.

It is not a matter of selecting particular passages which have wealth etc. for their subject, but a matter of seeing the gospel story as a whole through certain eyes.

10. p. 95 Yes, the Gospel is for everyone. But some will be able to embrace it more easily than others. The rich will be required to give up most. One cannot follow the Gospel and remain unchanged. That is the way of ideology and succumbing to "this world". You either read the

118

Gospel as one committed to social and economic change, or you don't.

11. p. 95   Perhaps it only falls short of a total Christian theology because we are used to thinking of a total Christian theology in a particular way. For those in oppression it *is total* because it is all they've got.

12. p. 96   You obviously have a horror of Marxist revolution. Perhaps you are right to have that. What is impossible to ignore, however, is the incisiveness of much Marxist analysis. I suspect one of the reasons why it is pilloried in the west is precisely its capacity to hit where it hurts the most. Liberation theologians in the West often say you can have Marxist analysis without being committed to a particular programme for the future, save that of finding a way to establish justice for all.

13. p. 98   Paul Tillich once suggested we substitute *separation* for sin. Sin is both a condition and an activity both individual and corporate.

14. p. 99   Though the main point about Christians being atheists was their refusal to sacrifice to the Emperor, who at that time was a divinely sanctioned ruler, or even divine himself.

15. p. 99   'Writes off' is a bit strong!

16. p. 99   I suppose Jesus was calling the righteous out of their righteousness. Now there's a message for religious people!

17. p. 100 *The Kingdom*: Its many dimensions have led scholars to wonder about where it is to be located — heaven or earth? — and when it comes — now or later?

Jesus probably envisaged very soon, and *on earth*. The fact it didn't happen led Luke's Gospel to postpone the event. But it would still be on *earth*, which would be wholly renewed at the second coming.

18. p. 100 The translation of 'humble': "good suggestion", and "yes it is" the same as marginalised non-people.

19. p. 100 *The poor*: A vague term including the disadvantaged, handicapped etc. etc., i.e. all those not included in the processes of society. Probably the power/powerless division is better than the rich/poor one. Liberation theology simply makes the connection between power and wealth, disadvantage and poverty.

20. p. 102 This is *not* a liberal assumption.

21. p. 104 In *The Absoluteness of Christianity* (1901, ET) Troeltsch did hold Christianity to be both relative and absolute i.e. superior. He did this by using an ethical criterion — Christianity was the most personalist of religions and had developed the business of personalist categories such as love to a greater degree than other religions. By the time he wrote his Oxford lecture (pub. 1923), he had researched other religions more and noted that they too had developed personalist love to a depth he had not known. Then he became relativist.

22. p. 105 For Hick there is also an epistemological argument, as well as the demythologising of the Incarnation.

119

23. p. 107 But you haven't told me why you can't (go along with Alan Race's position) so I'll still go along with my judgment.
24. p. 110 We understand the O.T. much less than we ought to. The tendency to blame the bad things in Christianity by saying they are O.T. remainders is scapegoating.
25. p. 110 Scholars are now saying that the newness of Jesus's teaching is deep-rooted in Judaism, and that there is nothing un-Jewish in his outlook.
26. p. 112 There are many ordained men in the Roman Catholic Church who wish to see women priests. U.S.A. and Holland are pushing the hardest.
27. p. 115 Part of the whole problem about women's ordination is, I think, this pedastalling of the Eucharist celebrant. The Eucharist is a communal celebration, not one man's party to which he invites guests.
28. p. 115 The Greek and Latin traditions were eqully patriarchal. Aristotle's female as 'misbegotten male' for example!
29. p. 116 Tradition has equated Mary Magdalene with the sinner of this ointment story. But it is probably a piece of myth-making.
30. p. 116 Presumably complementarity is different from complements of sexual stereotyping.
31. p. 117 All the better I would have thought!
32. p. 117 Both differentiationists and non-differentiationists cannot eschew women's ordination. The former for complementary reasons and the latter for 'a priori' reasons. Both seek to include women's experience and express it. Our problem is that we have made ordination the touchstone for expressing it. Which shows that the problem is about sex rather than ordination, in my view!.

YEAR III

Otterbourne

January 20, 1987

My dear E,

Well, sitting staring into space, cigarette in hand, and ready to light the next off the stub, has been my regular lot these last two and a half years. The syndrome of the blank page. But now it's worse, if that's possible. The time really has come to wrap it up.

The first problem I set myself was "to find out what modern Biblical scholarship (i.e. the Bishop of Durham amongst others) can tell the ordinary non-theologian about how Christianity began. What is historical fact? What is myth? Just like that. Imagine.

Looking back, I'm not sure what I was expecting. Was it a wholesale demolition job on the gospels which would be briskly written off as myth to leave us stranded by the ebbing tide on Don Cupitt's shore? Of course nothing of the sort transpired. I can't remember Leslie Houlden even mentioning the word "myth" in cold blood.

The liberal stance evolved in my own case from contemplation of the nature of the whole body of New Testament writing. It came as complete news to me. I think that in some obscure way I used to believe that the scriptures, accepted throughout the Church as the word of God, must therefore have been directly inspired by him, wielding the pen of the scribe like a ouija writer. The liberal blow was therefore struck in the opening lectures which rested squarely on the results of historical criticism. It dawned on me, as I wrote in the first paragraph of my first essay "that if the scriptures are indeed the word of God, they can simultaneously carry a perfectly rational human explanation. Why not?" Why not indeed? I was to find in subsequent reading pages thickly spattered with forced choices where none need exist. Human versus divine: God versus man: why set up these choices as mutually exclusive? Logically

121

impossible like a children's questionnaire. My standpoint is that many peeple's intellectual difficulties spring from a need to postulate dichotomies which need not be there. Because one is talking about entirely different levels of thinking and being.

I was equally amazed one evening when I asked how long these historical insights had been around. "About 200 years" was the answer. "Since the enlightenment." Good grief! I thought he would say about 50! Then how come we had failed to be enlightened? How come we didn't know? I think it is because we are an insular lot, not overkeen on foreign languages. This historical Biblical criticism, so rational and sensible, flourished as so much theology above all in Germany, and I suspect that it was not until Bultmann's *"Jesus Christ and Mythology"* was issued in English by the SCM in 1958 that these ideas obtained general currency in this country. Then look at the furore which greeted *'Honest to God'*, John Robinson's typically forthright reaction.

So, if we weren't taught that the Bible was just myth, what were we taught? Again looking back, I'm aware of enormous gaps in the material I relayed to you, and in the interests of achieving at least better balance and proportion, I think I ought to fill you in a bit on these.

We were made aware, for a start, of the basic lack of data on all fronts. Despite the fact that the New Testament writings constitute a uniquely numerous corpus of literature in the ancient world, we are left so often in frustrating ignorance. People flit in and out of the pages, mentioned once, of whom we know nothing at all. And this lack of data is pretty basic. Who *did* write the fourth gospel, Hebrews, Ephesians? If you are employing the method of historical criticism you have to consider carefully what the evidence will bear. And the critical tool appears to resemble nothing so much as the cryptography with which we are both familiar, assigning values to the gaps in the data.

I remember, earlier on, your writing fiercely to demand from me incontrovertible but simply non-existent evidence in relation to something or other. You then wondered what mention there is of Christianity in the classical writings of the period, thinking no doubt that this would be objective, uncorrupted. It is worth digressing to reply: the answer is — not much — but what there is, so interesting. It dates mostly from the second century, when the expanding movement seemed likely to threaten the empire.

Pliny the Younger was for a term governor of Bithynia in Northern Turkey, and about AD 110 wrote a fascinating letter to his friend the Emperor Trajan (*A new Eusebius* ed. J. Stevenson S.P.C.K. 1957), asking for advice on how to deal with these Christians. Should he get them to offer wine to the Gods, to curse Christ? Should he make them offer sacrifice to the Emperor's statue? (for by now the Emperors were held to be divine). The Christian threat (as before) was more political than religious. It is interesting that the epistle I Peter is addressed to this same community: it all constitutes the earliest known example of judicial processes being brought against Christians.

Both Tacitus and Suetonius made brief mention. Thus Tacitus, writing about AD 115 on Nero's persecution of the Christians in 64.

> "Christus, from whom the name had its origin, suffered the extreme penalty during the reign of Tiberius at the hands of one of our procurators, Pontius Pilate, and a deadly superstition, thus checked for the moment, again broke out not only in Judaea, the first source of the evil, but also in Rome, where all things hideous and shameful from every part of the world meet and become popular . . ."

And Suetonius, c.120 had (albeit mixed up)

> "Since the Jews constantly made disturbance at the instigation of Chrestus, he expelled them from Rome."
> (Life of Claudius)

and

> "Punishment was inflicted on the Christians, a class of men given to a new and wicked superstition."
> (Life of Nero)

The earliest reference occurs in the Jewish historian Josephus' *Jewish Antiquities*, of which you gave me a monumental volume of around 1870, the tiny print all but illegible. Alas, all scholars agree that this text has been got at by later Christians which is a pity, as Josephus died about 98 and would have been the earliest source. For what it's worth, I give the passage. (*Jewish Antiquities* Bk XVIII. CH. III 3.3) from your edition.

> "Now there was about this time, Jesus, a wise man, if it be lawful to call him a man, for he was a doer of wonderful works — a teacher of such men as receive the truth with pleasure. He drew over to him both many of the Jews, and many of the Gentiles. He was (the) Christ; and when Pilate, at the suggestion of the principal men amongst us, had condemned him to the cross, those that loved him at the first did not forsake him, for he appeared to them live again the third day, as the divine prophets had foretold these and ten thousand other wonderful things concerning him; and the tribe of Christians, so named from him, are not extinct at this day."

So there you are. Slight, few, and except for Josephus, authentic fragments of classical history, which I hope you feel were worth the digression. I discovered them after you wrote.

We were talking, when I broke off, about the ever-recurring frustration of inadequate data, and though it would be tedious to enumerate many examples, here are a few to give substance to the point.

After Jesus' arrest, all his disciples left him and ran away and "a certain young man dressed only in a linen cloth, was following Jesus. They tried to arrest him, but he ran away naked leaving the cloth behind". (Mark 14: 51, 52.) Was this Mark himself, as tradition asserts? A charming intelligent Japanese lady in our class was the one who asked this. And Leslie Houlden replied, as always "We don't know", and suggested other ways of interpreting the passage.

More about Mark. The Roman Catholic teacher Etienne Charpentier on whose "*How to read the New Testament*" I have leaned heavily, asserts that this gospel is almost certainly based on the preaching of Peter. His source is Papias, early second century Bishop, who wrote

"Mark was an interpreter of Peter and wrote down carefully what he remembered — though not in order — of what was said or done by the Lord. He had in fact neither heard the Lord or followed him, but later on, as I said, he followed Peter — ".

But in our lecture we heard that Papias is not a reliable witness: when checkable he proves wrong. So one has to suspend judgment.

Perhaps most tantalising is our ignorance of the relationship between John, son of Zebedee: the Beloved Disciple: the author(s) of the Fourth Gospel; and the Johannine community. Are any of these identical? If so, how many? In any event, Leslie Houlden told us that at the end of the day there is no worthwhile information about how the Fourth Gospel was written and who wrote it. Nor is it known where it was written: possibly Alexandria or Ephesus. Remember (from my first essay), that it was circulating in Egypt by about AD 120. Nor does the gospel even mention the apostle... Yet while promulgating due caution, our tutor at the same time recommended *The Community of the Beloved Disciple*" by the Catholic theologian Raymond Brown. Professor Brown constructs and describes an entire community around the person of the Beloved Disciple, and ascribes to it the eventual authorship of the gospel in around AD 90. But he himself warns his reader that his reconstruction claims at most probability; and if sixty per cent of his detective work is accepted he will be happy, he says.

We also touched on the question of the manuscripts, as I have in passing. Another fertile breeding ground for uncertainty, you might suppose, literally thousands of manuscripts copied in early times by enthusiastic amateurs, and later by monk scribes in their monasteries. I like to picture Boccaccio, author of the Decameron, ferreting about in dusty monastic libraries to rescue some of these manuscripts, for that is what he did.

Of course the texts were difficult. Pronouns could sound the same in dictation so that you had to guess from the sense whether 'you' or 'we' was intended — a feature I seem to remember from my own schooldays, if the verb-ending clue was absent or corrupt in any way. Attributions were affected by the style of the Greek. Paul wrote in such and such a way normally via his amanuensis. Could he just change his style? — Ephesians is so different. That sort of consideration.

Then there are discrepancies such as the ending of Mark. The earliest manuscripts stop at 16: 8, abruptly and extraordinarily, the women running away terrified from the empty tomb and telling nobody. All scholars now agree that verses 16: 9-20, detailing resurrection appearances, are later interpolations because they did not appear in the best early manuscripts. Other examples appear in all the other N.T. books, mostly much less arresting. Then there were occasional scribes, who would add bits of their own, but easily spotted. Again, scribes might suggest alternatives in the margin and their successors would incorporate them in the text. But we understood that given the magnitude of the copying task as a whole, the surprising thing is that the textual variations and discrepancies amount to so little and are doctrinally so unimportant. The important uncertainties evidently lie elsewhere.

The supremely important question is of course how much we know for certain about Jesus himself. And apart from general knowledge of first century Palestine, our only means of knowing is, in J.L.H.'s vivid phrase, by 'interrogating' the gospels. Two years ago I felt that I had somehow established contact with Paul better than with them, so I've been trying to get to grips with them again. Plenty of uncertainty here: dating, authorship and relation to each other for starters. And, in fact, their general character. As to this, it is unanimously agreed that they are not contemporary eye-witness accounts, albeit possibly based on these, the earliest (generally considered to be Mark as we saw) written some thirty to forty years after the crucifixion. Further, they are not biographies concerned with the modern historian's passion for so-called objective truth. They are not trying to prove the truth of Christianity as in a logic lesson (which I know well by now I can't do to you, my dear E). The evangelists knew it already by other means, and their passionate concern was to guard and pass on their supremely good news. Thus all we've got is secondary rather than primary evidence for Jesus offering plenty of scope for historical uncertainty.

As to the main character of all the gospels, their common

heritage is that they are based on oral tradition, on stories going the rounds. But each gospel is written from each evangelist's own theological viewpoint — modern scholarship is very keen on this idea. And this means that *interpretation is built in from the start*. It's easier to see with an example, as follows — One of the biggest puzzles is how Jesus regarded himself. Perhaps a clue lies in the following. To be ignorant is to be human. Perhaps Jesus didn't know he was God because he was human, yet there is a paradox here according to which gospel you take. The 'My God, why hast thou forsaken me' of Mark betokens a Jesus for whom perfect trust in God represented a very human endeavour complete with uncertainty. But all the "He in me and I in him" language of the Fourth Gospel indicates a very different relationship which ends up in the creeds. In any event, if the evangelists themselves are interpreting, so may we.

On the specific questions of dating, authorship and relationship to each other — reams and reams have been written, book after book. This is very briefly what I hoisted on board.

As long ago as 1780 a theologian called Griesbach established the synoptic problem by lining up different gospel episodes in columns of three and seeing what he got. He believed that Matthew came first, then Luke, and finally Mark providing the synopsis from which the name of the problem arose. (John has always been out on its own.) Then lo and behold in our own day comes John Robinson's thesis seeking to prove that John came first. When I stayed with the Maxwell-Hyslops, they had just devoured him from cover to cover. Also I gather that your Treasury friend is about to devote years of his retirement to proving the same thing. Meanwhile it is the generally accepted view that Mark did indeed come first, and it was to Mark, presumed therefore to be the most authentic source, that nineteenth century agnostics turned in their fruitless search for the Jesus of history.

And what of their inter-relationship? It is generally accepted that both Matthew and Luke appear to have drawn heavily on Mark and we were given fascinating statistical detail on this, viz — that of the 661 verses of which Matthew consists, only 65 are not to be found in Mark: Luke took about 3/5 of Mark: only about

1/3 of Mark is not in both Matthew and Luke, and so on. But this left a further difficulty: both Matthew and Luke include matter *not* found in Mark. Whence did it come? From Q = Quelle = German for source — a quite unverifiable hypothesis in turn challenged by John Drury (amongst others) in his work on Luke. But all speculative — We simply don't know and probably never shall.

Perhaps I have been overstressing the uncertainty factor. Theologians do believe they can detect elements of greater authenticity in relation to Jesus. They cite for instance the prominence accorded in the synoptics to Jesus' preaching on the Kingdom of God, a phrase which was probably not so central to the Judaism of that day though the idea behind it was well established. (Here again one sees the value of historical criticism in presenting us with this knowledge.) Then there was Jesus' unconditional acceptance of outcasts. There is absolutely no reason to think that the early church of the later first century was keen enough on outcasts to have invented them and put them in unless Jesus himself had shown his concern in word and deed for outcasts of all sorts. The call to repentance, however, was not unique but common to all the prophets and in full accordance with the times. Above all, Jesus' emphasis on his coming suffering and death, and its occurrence as surely a purposed and not unexpected event, is seen as a playing out of the central doctrinal theme that death is the clue to life. Between Jesus' preaching and his living, word and deed, there was no difference but an integrity. This comes over in all the gospels.

What else did we learn? All sorts of odds and ends, not proving anything but helping to build a total picture. We were given the fruit of a great deal of close detective work which examined the differences between the gospels, for example in their choice (if it was choice) of material. Had you realised that the birth stories occurred only in Matthew and Luke? The shepherds only in Luke? The flight into Egypt and the slaughter of the Innocents only in Matthew? Did you know of the discrepancy in the naming of the twelve, and Nathaniel appearing in John and nowhere else. But if one asks: How come? Why these discrepancies? Why the different stories? Did each evangelist know of their existence or did he choose to omit them? — the answer again is a blank: We simply don't know, though stories in one Gospel sometimes bear strong marks of that evangelist's style and vocabulary.

One could go on in this vein, studying the orders in which the stories are given (by no means necessarily chronological), the choice of linking adverbs, seminal words such as that for rending the heavens so that God could shout through (Mark 1: 10 and 15: 38; Matthew 27: 51), the passage in John (14: 31) where Jesus says 'Come, let us go hence' but in point of fact they don't go at all, another discourse follows, which is held to be evidence of slipshod editing. And another arresting item, of comfort to high Christologists, Jesus is spoken of in John as being 'sent' by the Father no less than 40 times. These are the things one remembers.

Another way, a traditional way, of studying Christology has been to extract evey ounce of meaning and significance from the 'titles' bestowed on Jesus by himself and others. 'Son of man', 'Son of God', 'Messiah', 'Christ', 'Adam', 'Lord'. This is a very scholastic exercise and I can't say I find it illuminating. What I do remember, without looking it up, is that 'Son of God' had absolutely nothing whatever to do with the virgin birth but was already in use in the Old Testament for angels, kings, and, in due course, faithful servants of God; and that *Kirios* was a common mode of address and besides Lord, could mean nothing more than Sir — Hi Mister as indeed today. Shades of Greek holidays! All these terms developed in the richness of their sense through their application to Jesus, seen as God's emissary.

To many people besides you and me the Fourth Gospel is a different matter altogether. It used to be thought, I believe, that the *logos* idea was largely responsible and said particular things to particular people fortunate enough to have enjoyed a classical education. These included Clement of Alexandria (late second century) who said that the synoptics were for simple souls, while the Fourth Gospel was suitable for spiritual people like him. Many followed him, including Dean Inge, C.H. Dodd and all who could gleefully detect Greek thought in the background — which includes me!

129

However, we understood that partly as a result of the discovery of the Dead Sea Scrolls — don't ask me what they said — there is now a swing away from this view to recognition that John owes more to a Jewish background and that the *logos* concept is prefectly compatible with certain strands in Judaism reaching back to Genesis and on to the Wisdom of Solomon. The truth of the matter, says J.L.H., is that by now Judaism was heavily penetrated by Hellenistic thought. Remember the ossuaries.

But this letter is meant to be a summing up — bolstered, I fear, with bits of fresh material which have somehow escaped earlier essays and yet are very germane to the main thesis.

Which is — in my view — the extent of uncertainty and interpretation from the word go, Paul and the evangelists all viewing Jesus from their own not necessarily compatible perspectives, but agreeing wholly on his centrality. We realised the impossibility of uncovering the Jesus of history. We learnt many interesting facts, some pointing one way, some the other. For instance, the penetration into all contemporary religious thought of Eastern mystery cults, some including virgin births (but I knew about these already from my archaelogist friend Rachel Maxwell-Hyslop). On the other hand, there were these many mentions of God 'sending' his son into the world, as already mentioned. But never was it said — this is myth. We were left, assorted lot that we were, to make up our own minds.

Time for a break in the scripture lesson! And for a very good cause, namely to hear John Lill playing *two* Beethoven piano concertos. (Their relevance comes later.) Also to see where my puss has got to. I find her in her favourite new spot, perched on the windowsill in my bedroom, warming her tail on the radiator and gazing out over the snowy waste of the common. Margot, fetching Laura from school, said she looked up to find herself *transfixed* by this penetrating green stare.

On to our second year on Doctrine which was a very different matter, ranging far and wide, also exponential and historical, reviewing the attempts through the ages at this very interpretation. (Here I owe Alan Race an apology. His 'reams of printed material', including quotes, poetry, diagrams, have proved invaluable.)

For me, as I think you understand, the salient experience was reading Bultmann, that tiny little treatise picked up out of our London University Extension Courses book-box almost at random. I wrote quite a lot about it last year so won't repeat myself; and for the first time I detected a measure of agreement in your reply (12 Nov. 1985). But I have been thinking about it since, and consider that not enough has been made of the positive side of Bultmann's theses — viz., the importance of existential encounter and the need to demythologise. If much of the gospels *is* mythological, not literal, in its cosmic framework this would be — *is* — to many people a shattering thought. I understand now very well why preachers daren't touch it with a barge-pole. But existentialism can fill the gap, making us aware by analogy from human love and friendship to the nature of divine love and friendship. Opening up areas of experience of, in this world incomparable beauty and delight. Indeed, we agreed on that too. I can think of other illustrations too. A friend of mine was studying for her Ph.D. the effects of certain treatments, including all sorts of high-tec., on certain categories of disabled people. I kept interrogating her on the progress of her research and finally demanded to know her main conclusion. "That people need people", she replied. And from my job running the British Institute of Industrial Therapy I call to mind many, many of our workshop manager members and the affectionate way they looked after their mentally and physically disabled work-forces. Person to person encounter, without fore thought or after thought — is what I'm on about. Translated into theology, it helps to remove (alongside the liberation concept) our great salvation obstacle, our antipathy to the idea of *winning* salvation by good works. As a child I was positively alarmed at the prospect of heaven portrayed by the Victorian hymn-writers: 'Once in Royal David's City', so admirable in other respects, finishes:

"Where like stars his children crowned
All in white shall wait around."

What a listless prospect! But existential encounter with someone whose service is perfect freedom, that's a different matter.

131

Needless to say there was a great deal more to the Doctrine course than Rudolf Bultmann. To follow up all the leads we were given would take a lifetime, and even to come up with an essay or two I found hard work and time-consumeing.

But I feel I must round this off with something on the Christological problem. You yourself earlier in our correspondence stated this in forceful modern prose — not the first to do so. Everyone from earliest times has been stumped and every attempt at too specific definitions seems to run into trouble. Docetists believed that Christ's body only appeared to be human — he really remained God all the time. Arians that he never was fully divine. Gnostics, believing a variety of things, sought enlightenment through esoteric spiritual mysteries. And so on. All were declared heretical (which we no longer mind about). Eventually in AD 451, the date of the Council of Chalcedon, the following appeared to meet with satisfaction:

> "We confess one and the same our Lord Jesus Christ, the same perfect in godhead, the same perfect in manhood, truly God and truly man, the same of a rational soul and body . . . acknowledged in two natures without confusion, without change, without division, without separation, the difference of the natures being by no means taken away because of the union, but rather, the distinctive character of each nature being preserved and combining in the person or entity."

An adjoining part of the Definition comes in the 'History of Christianity' by Paul Johnson (p. 92) which you gave me for Christmas. Equally obscure. No wonder the Bishops of the Church of England, confronted with a similar task (The Nature of Christian Belief. Church House Publishing. 1986) are also barely intelligible. You can't define a mystery. That's what a mystery is.

Do you want to know what I think? It is that by concentrating on what the evidence will bear, and on the historical settings against which Biblical events and writings unfold, you get a position not as iconoclastic as the out and out myth-mongers, but certainly a thousand miles removed from the fundamentalists.

And is a myth such an inadequate thing? I have been re-

reading my notes on Bultmann, and really he *does* make acceptable sense. Let me finish with two definitions, one (his) at the height of perceptive theology, the other at a more workaday level. Bultmann: "It may be said that myths give to the transcendant reality an immanent, this-worldly objectivity ('Der Mythos objectiviert das Jenseitige zum Diessitigen')". The other I came across in Thomas Kenneally's 'Schindler's Ark' that brilliant Booker Prize-winning novel, based on fact, about a German businessman rescuing Jews from Auschwitz (p. 227).

"For the thing about a myth is not whether it is true or not, nor whether it *should* be true, but that it is somehow truer than truth itself."

Personally, I can live quite happily on a mixture of these two ideas.

Love as ever,
Nancy.

26 January 1987

My dear Nancy,

Many thanks for the latest effort returned herewith with a few pencilled scrawls for whatever they're worth. I think it reads fluently and well. And I feel it's at the centre of theological problems. There, though, I can't find anything to get my teeth into, somehow: Theology is a sort of doughnut, as I see it. Not my cup of tea either. I'm lost if there's no question of fact and inference, and not all that clearly located even when there is.

Love as ever,
E.

10 January. Otterbourne

My dear E,

One of my subsidiary objects in undertaking these courses was to see if they threw any light on the science/religion dichotomy as it now stands. See introduction. Well, it wasn't to be expected that the subject would come within shouting distance of analyses of the New Testament. But what about Doctrine? Nature of God? Nature of reality? I promised myself another go

133

at these matters once the bustle of term-times, the tyranny of essays, were behind me. There would be the opportunity for unhurried reading and uninterrupted reflection.

Not a hope! I'm just not capable. I bought two paper backs by two top-accredited physicists J.C. Polkinghorne and Paul Davies, purporting to make all clear — or as clear as it can be made — to the general reader. What *is* clear is that I don't even qualify for that: The minute I spy an equation I run for cover, and as to the text I'm unable to remember from one moment to the other any difference between neutron, electron and quark. The only thing to do in these circumstances is to look at any preface or introduction in which the author spells out what he proposes to write about, then the conclusion when he tells you what he *has* written about, and take the middle as read!

Which I've done, turning back at the same time to our correspondence of February 1986. This has been rather satisfactory so far as I'm concerned. On the subject of Heisenberg's uncertainty principle, whereby we can measure either the position or the velocity of a particle, you wrote: "I take this to concern the nature of measurement, not the nature of reality." Let me refer you to the last chapter of Polkinghorne's *"The Quantum World"* entitled (mercifully) 'What does it mean?' You my dear E, in what you say, apparently follow the founding father Bohr's Copenhagen school, with its emphasis on measuring instruments, and its preferences for thinking of quantum theory simply as calculational procedure.

> "But", writes Polkinghorne, "if in the end science is just about the harmonious reconciliation of the behaviour of laboratory apparatus, it is hard to see why it is worth the expenditure of effort involved. I have never known anyone working in fundamental science who was not motivated by the desire to understand the way the world is." (p. 79.)

And he goes on to propose that the objective approach, the positing of an objective world which the scientist by successive discoveries gradually lays bare, seems to offer the more fruitful line. The only trouble is that what is laid bare is no longer the solid certainty of nineteenth century billiard-ball physics, but the uncertainty, the unpredictability, the mere probability and potentiality of the new quantum mechanical world. In the words of Heisenberg himself, also quoted (p. 81) —

> "In the experiments about atomic events we have to do with things and facts, with phenomena which are just as real as any phenomena in daily life. But the atoms or elementary particles are not as real: they form a world of potentialities or possibilities rather than one of things or facts."

I think this is as far as I can go on this subject — probably further. Obviously, as we agreed before, nothing is to be gained by trying to equate God with mental constructs in molecular physics. But the state of the art is an advance on the headlong clash between matter and mind which characterised science/religion relationships in the last century.

So far we have been talking about the effect of quantum theory on the structure of the atom and its infinitely tiny constituent particles. But the new physics has also of course plenty to say about the physical world at the other end of the scale, namely, cosmology. Creation. The big bang and all that. Last night (Jan 11, '87 BBC2 Everyman) our heroes were talking about the old Big Bang and the new Big Bang. (Were you aware that the origingal Big Bang is such old hat that it has been already superseded? But I'm not sure by what?)

What quantum mechanical cosmology boils down to, so far as I can make out, is that the universe may now, in their delightful terminology, be thought of as a 'free lunch', something for or from nothing. Let me quote Paul Davies (p. 216).

> "In this remarkable scenario, the entire cosmos simply comes out of nowhere, completely in accordance with the laws of quantum physics, and creates along the way all the matter and energy needed to build the universe we now see. It thus incorporates the creation of all physical things, including space and time. Rather than postulate an unknowable singularity to start the universe off, the quantum space-time model attempts to explain everything entirely within the context of the laws of physics. It is an awesome claim. We are used to the idea of 'putting something in and getting something out' but getting something for nothing (or out of nothing) is alien. Yet the

world of quantum physics routinely produces something for nothing. Quantum gravity suggests we might get everything for nothing."

What we are interested in is whether this theory (if true) squeezes God, yet again, out of the picture? If he is no longer required even to press the button, why postulate his existence? And the answer seems to be: We need to postulate his existence in order to fix the quantum principles by which all this takes place.

Davies again (still p. 16):

> "Physics can perhaps explain the content, origin and organisation of the physical universe, but not the laws (or superlaws) of physics itself. Traditionally God is credited with having invented the laws of nature and created the things (space-time, atoms, people among others) on which these laws operate. The 'free lunch' scenario claims that all you need are the laws — the universe can take care of itself, including its own creation."

This type of thinking promotes the concept of God even more decisively in the direction of mind, to a reality so little involved in the detail of the physical world as not even being required to set it off. Yet there is plenty of Biblical support for this idea too. 'God is a spirit and they that worship him must worship him in spirit and in truth.'

Which brings us back to the more poetic way of envisaging the creation already quoted (p. 81) that of Simone Weil. Her thesis, you will remember, is that the very act of creation involves separation, despite the fact that there remains in it, for ever, so much of yourself. When you have created something you let it go. That's it. You are not required to keep digging up the roots to see how it is getting on. All creative artists I'm sure will at this point rise to their feet to applaud this view, from their own deep experience.

I think there is an analogy here between creating and giving. If you give somebody something, that's it. If you give a nephew a tip for Christmas, you may express the hope that he will spend it on x, y or z, but it's up to him to decide. That is, if it's genuine free money, not a token with strings attached.

My old grandmother had not entirely grasped this principle, I remember, any more than she had mastered the general art of giving. People who served her in various capacities often found themselves contemplating a tooled leather blotter, acquired in foreign parts, when something much more mundane would have been acceptable. But I digress.

I'm not sure this is very helpful as a conclusion. The reason why I've gone into all this, I have to keep reminding myself, is *not* to investigate scientific explanations for the presence or absence of God in the universe (though you may be forgiven for having thought so). It is to draw a comparison between the theologian's and the scientist's frame of mind when contemplating these matters. And I have to report that I find them congruent.

That is, the new physicist congruent with the new (liberal) theologian. For this reason I cannot accept Paul Davies' proposed antithesis, when he designates the theological viewpoint thus (p. 220):

> "Religion is founded on dogma and received wisdom which purports to represent immutable truth."

Well, this may be true of dogmatic theology, but liberal theology leaves us more room for manoeuvre by positively requiring that the interpretative faculty be exercised. That's its great beauty. One feels one need no longer get pinned down, shot up, or whatever, by any scientific discovery whatsoever, as was the fate of the church confronted by Galileo. The God I worship, immortal, invisible, God only wise, is at once out of reach of such disaster and yet still always accessible because of the incarnation.

Love
Nancy

30 January 1987

My dear Nancy,

Back in rural Essex, with your latest thoughts in store to warm the winter's cold. You'll forgive me if I'm a bit flummoxed by a god who invents the basic principles of physics, waits a billion years, and then injects Jesus. It suggests at least a change of mind, and indeed heart. It's clear to me that the universe is already quite mysterious enough, not to say impossible, even before we confuse it still further by seeking to explain it. Perhaps we can do no better than striving to cultivate our gardens, as Voltaire said. I've always quite enjoyed that.

Love as ever,
Yours E.

Otterbourne

Jan. 27, 28, 29, 1987

My dear E,

Another reason why I wanted to do these courses, was to see what they had to say on the subject of Race relations (Ho! Ho! as John Timpson used to say) — Christianity in relation to other faiths. Then I did a whole essay on it, fairly recently too, and I have to say, I fear, that I haven't made much progress since. However, I'll take up where I left off, and report where I have got to.

I wrote (p. 107):

> "but at the end of the day it seems to me one has to retain Christ as defining the difference between good and evil, no matter what the content of other religions may be. I can't go along with Alan Race in stigmatising this position as unjustified theological imperialism!"

In the margin Alan Race wrote his tutor's comment "but you haven't told me why you can't: so I'll still go along with my judgment." And what this judgment means, of course is that to Alan all religions are equally valid.[1] His position seems to be the ultimate relativism. I suppose you think that too, arriving there from the opposite pole and probably (if I know you) calling them all equally *in*valid.

You may not believe it, but struggling to decide what *I* think has cast me into a state of turmoil for three days. Puffing

138

furiously, and as you know I'm a non-smoker except on these occasions. And finally what I've come up with is a split between Christianity and Christ — not a cheap hit but a way of sorting out different considerations. Let me explain: I agree with Alan that historically the Church has been imperialistic. But I disagree that Jesus himself was, or could be interpreted as having been.[2]

For historically from the viewpoint of a non-Christian, Christianity must have looked triumphalistic, superior, imperialistic, the lot. It has also perpetrated a good deal of appalling violence. It has done this both when engaging in missionary activity and also, closer home, when it has striven for too close a (theological) definition when alternatives have had their protagonists. Latest example, dug up from Paul Johnson's History of Christianity, that the Roman and Orthodox branches of the Church split over inserting the word *filioque* in the creed to denote that the Holy Spirit proceeds from the Son as well as the Father. See what I mean? So Christianity has been violent and imperialist — and still is, in certain insensitive missionary endeavours reported recently in the press.

To switch from the history of Christianity (rather abbreviated!) to the founder of Christianity gives a quite different feel. One jibs at the language to start with: 'superior'. I know it is perfectly OK technically, just as the word 'prior' is OK but sounds peculiar away from the printed page where it belongs. But surely the Jesus who washed the disciples' feet would have had none of it.

On to more philosophical, linguistic and translating considerations which some scholars invoke in order to make the concept of Christ's finality more acceptable to those of other faiths. I already mentioned that no problem arises if the incarnation is regarded as myth — the Hick position. Then the point has been made that all the 'one and only' adjectives used to describe Jesus belong 'not to the language of philosophy, science or dogmatics but rather to the language of confession and testimony' . . . New Testament authors employ the language not of scientists but of lovers — like 'You are the only girl in the world for me', and so on. This is quite a powerful point, taken in connection with all we have learnt about the nature of the New

Testament.

Then a point of translation appeals to me. In the original Greek for *Son of God*, the definitive article 'the' does not appear and the epithet could equally well be translated as 'a' *Son of God*. The thrust of the argument is that certain passages now enshrined as philosophical evidence for Christ's exclusivity were originally never so intended. (Knitter. p. 182 et seq.) The consequence of these re-interpretations, when engaging in dialogue with those of other faiths, is obvious. According to Knitter, such readings do not lessen the need for total commitment; it must be just as total, but wider.

I thought you caught the point exactly a few letters back with your transmitter analogy.

Now I want to dodge back to history — for this letter is not a taut argument but a collection of more or less fruitful ideas. Coming into the category of *more* fruitful is the following, which emanates from the ever fertile mind of Karl Rahner, so I understand. He views the history of Christianity in three stages: the first, Judaistic, was the church as first established in the earliest period of the New Testament: the second transformed into Roman, European and Western culture — the 'Roman Captivity' as it has been called. And the third stage will see it becoming a truly world church, truly Catholic in the broadest sense and in dialogue with Islam and the Eastern religions. In the words of Raimundo Panikkar —

> "The almost self-evident fact is that the Western-Christian tradition seems to be exhausted, I might almost say effete, when it tries to express the Christian message in a meaningful way for our times."

And suddenly one thinks of Terry Waite who, surely all would agree, *does* express the Christian message in a meaningful way for our times. And there are two vital ingredients in his make-up. One is that his mission is *humanitarian*: if one of the hostages turned out to hold different religious beliefs from his or none at all, one can't imagine that would weigh at all with Terry Waite. The second strong weapon in his armoury is his knowledge of Islam — a deep knowledge, one gathers. Without it he would not know where to begin.

My own view, for what it's worth, is coloured by my relativist ideas on perception and apprehension — the relativity of all knowledge. This applies of course also to religious knowledge so that we cannot know the nature of Christ in all his fulness — his 'superiority' or otherwise, simply by making philosophical statements about it. The only way we can know is by doing his will, the old-fashioned way of expressing the concept of the priority of *praxis*. And on that pilgrims' way, the experience is that we meet people of other faiths or none, also, surprise, surprise, travelling the same road and succouring the same casualties by the wayside. In other words, practice, praxis, experience happen first. Then comes interpretation. After all, it took 400 years to come up with the Chalcedonian definition. It may well be that any church of exclusivist mentality, dragging its heels, will find itself outrun by events.

Love
Nancy

Otterbourne

Jan. 31 et seq. 1987

My dear E,

Glad you like my Spoonerism (My dear friend Valery's son scored porn on someone's ideas). I am assured it is authentically spontaneous. You ask if I think it is true that 'that elderly cleric celebrated Queen Victoria's Diamond Jubilee procession with glad cries of "three cheers for the queer old Dean!" ' I have to say 'No: that old chestnut sounds to me too contrived for that!'

Back to work and consideration of the last question I asked myself in the Introduction two and a half years ago.

> "Aim to discover how it can come about that two old friends of the same twentieth century Oxbridge culture can hold totally opposing views on the validity of the Christian faith and yet arrive at a close consensus on operational values."

I have left it till last because it is the crunch question. If I cannot answer it, or if the answer is unsatisfactory, then in a very real sense Christianity is out for me. Taking our friendship and common sense of values simply as an example of the thousands of other life-enhancing relationships (I think life-enhancing is Bernard Berenson, usually applied to Renaissance painting) which occur all over the world, over equally fundamental divides — it is a matter of common simple experience that they are a Good Thing. If (my apprehension of) Christianity cannot accommodate them then (my apprehension of) Christianity is at fault and must change so that it *can* accommodate them. This is not so sacriligious as might be supposed. No less a person than John Taylor, former Bishop of Winchester, says it has long been his conviction that God is not hugely concerned as to whether we are religious or not. (*A matter of life and death* SCM 1986 p. 18.) In other words, what he (I think) and I (certainly) understand by the idea of God must be such as to embrace the religious and the non-religious, Catholics, Protestants, Atheists, Muslims, Hindus and the whole galaxy of Karl Rahner's 'anonymous Christians' — together with every life-enhancing relationship between them.

All I have to do now is tell you how I personally arrive at this position, and see if it satisfies you.

I do it by regarding God as the highest value.

"Well, what's very remarkable about that?" I can hear you saying. "Sounds like Aquinas and Abelard again and I thought we'd dealt with them. You'll have to expand on the idea before one can tell if there is any merit in it, before one can tell whether one can be a Christian and an atheist with equal satisfaction to all concerned — especially God (assuming for one moment there *is* a God)."

The first step in the argument is to state that there is no such thing as apprehensible objective reality. (I know that's not a very original idea either, but then after three thousand years of Western philosophy there are no *new* ideas, only re-hashes.) To re-cap: this is true in at least three disciplines, quite unlikely bed-fellows. I must say I was tremendously excited when trying to grasp molecular physics, to be told that it all boiled down, or rather atoms all split up, into probabilities. Then there is another field which I've only just thought of as being a discipline where this also holds good, namely statistics, and social science. I doubt if any statistician or social scientist would have much truck with absolute truth or objective reality. He works with

142

probability theory, correlations, indices, all of which achieve a high degree of certainty depending on the material to hand and the sophistication of the methodology, but all of which at the end of the day can only show *indirectly* the way things are.

Thus fortified, one can turn with a glad cry to theology. If God cannot be apprehended totally, it is evident that each individual can only see him in his own terms and in the historical setting in which he is, however much and rightly he combines with others in church institutions for worship and support. The kind of language in vogue today recognises this in every field: "In terms of": "Weatherwise"; "It all depends what you mean by": Objective reality in its most humdrum guises is meaningless unless viewed as being in relation to something or other. In theology, we have seen how this works out in New Testament study. Each gospel, each epistle, embodies the writer's own interpretation of the person of Christ. In each case the material is selected and written up with a particular purpose in mind. It is not, so to speak, cast formless upon the waters.

We can go forward (or back) into history and follow this thinking through, noticing how the Church tends to conservatism because it is slow to re-interpret. Indeed, we *did* go back in history, some time ago, and noted the historical and poetic record of a nomadic tribe which constitutes the Old Testament. We noted primitive ideas of Divinity, more like the pagan Jove hurling his thunderbolts from Mount Olympus, and making pacts with humans, than of the Christian God. And since we cannot postulate that it is God who changes (or can we, if we are process theologians?) — then it must be our ideas of him which have to change.

So far we have been talking about cognitive knowlege, propositionally expressed. But it has often occurred to me to wonder whether one could not extend it to other types of perception including the mystical. Surely mystical experience too is culturally and historically affected since it can only be given to the (culturally affected) human recipient. Thus those who see visions of the Virgin Mary moving about on her plinth have to be Roman Catholic, since only the members of this confession accord her a status capable of doing such things. You yourself asked a rhetorical question in the words of a tabloid

143

headline — "Was it the Virgin Mary Mrs. O'Reilly saw from her scullery window?" You said No. I say 'Maybe, if she was a Catholic'. And to pursue the theme: I feel sure that the Yugoslav peasant children who saw the most recent famous visions could never have been little Protestants. All this would mean that the sub-conscious as well as the conscious proposition-forming mind is historically and culturally affected.

Does it also mean (one has to ask) that God is a purely subjective concept? No, I don't think this need follow, remembering that the very concept of relativity itself only derives meaning from the concept of the Absolute. (Whale, I believe.) And that experience had to be *of* something. All it means, I repeat, is that the God of Christianity, Judaism, Islam and so on can only be apprehended in the conceptual framework which determines the seeker's thinking.

I've plugged this *ad nauseum*, but it does leave us free to regard God as the highest value. To me. I hope to us. It doesn't mean that he may not also possess all the other attributes credited to him — 'Immortal, invisible' 'Eternal Father' — 'God whose almighty word', are only some of Hymns Ancient and Modern first lines proclaiming these sentiments — for there is no end to his modes of being and of being apprehended. Just, modestly, that so to designate him now helpfully corresponds to our requirements of oecumenism and art. And if that can seem too free-booting, I hope to point to the truth of the incarnation (not necessarily its literal truth), as indicating the positively top-most value by which all else may be judged. The normative aspect of Christ in technical language.

The idea of God as highest value is not new to me. I must have held it since I was about eight. It was then that my first crisis of faith occurred, for I realised that cricket had not been invented in the time of our Lord. And that therefore Jesus could not have been the best batsman, with the finest cover drive, that the world has ever known. Wasn't that a shattering discovery? By the cricket-crazed small girl, whose exercise books were thick with doodles of flannelled fieldsmen out on the boundary, backs to us, legs planted firmly astride to render them manifestly unready for the unlikely catch — because that was the only way I could draw them.

Updated somewhat, the idea now appeals because this way one can include art as something possessing top value — beauty to accompany the truth and goodness which are already often subsumed in our ideas of the nature of God. In fact the idea seems to chime well, for men have readily and blindly dedicated their lives to art as to religious faith. And yet the artefacts they produce are undoubtedly relative in the sense that tastes are forever changing. Just as, in liberal theology, our ideas of God's truth and goodness are always changing on account of the relativism and historicity of our perceptions. Nor of course are we confined to art. This value is discernible in all the activities of man from engineering to buying and selling to music-making. It just is that creative artists seem specially at risk of encountering God as they aim to express the highest values of which they are capable, subordinating all else to their art. (An aside. Isn't it criminal to deny to bright children the opportunity to strive for excellence?)

If we are to have highest value, we must accompany this with value judgments and I have something to say about these too. It is this, the fact that value judgments have no place in scientific and statistical analysis has been wrongly extrapolated to affirm that value judgments should not be made at all. I heard an extraordinary instance of this on the radio some time ago. A recovering heroin addict, member of a therapeutic group, was being interviewed.

Interviewer — Aren't you just as dependent on this community as you were on heroin?

Interviewee — What a funny question! Perhaps I am. But here it is *good* for me.

In other words, the interviewer was quite impervious to a value judgment of *goodness*. So we have the permissive, unjudged society, whereas we ought to be making value judgments practically every moment of our lives. How else does one live? How else, in the old phrase, is one captain of one's soul? This is supposing one intends to live one's life and not be forever side-tracked by circumstance and the value judgments of others less lily-livered than oneself.

On to the last lap, which overlaps with my preceding section

145

on Christianity and other faiths. If you are to have God as highest value, you have to have a touchstone by which to distinguish hierarchies of values. My view, which brings us neatly back to the heart of the theological debate, is that Christ himself incarnate or not, myth or not, provides this touchstone by living a life, and dying a death which were immediately perceived as exemplifying this new cast iron quality of excellence. I know there is a movement afoot in theological circles aimed at showing how much Jesus owed to Judaism. But I say, why did he *bother* to give us the new love commandment if the decalogue was enough. This is the crux of the matter. Jesus' value-system, Judaic in origin certainly, yet provides because of this one new commandment the touchstone by which one recognises a value so high that it equates with God.

Love
Nancy

7 February 1987

Dear Nancy,

For some reason I can't concentrate on the trivial pursuits that usually preoccupy me; so I turn to the profundities of theology as a welcome diversion. And instantly I'm plunged into my usual stupefaction; I can't even understand the basic vocabulary, let alone the questions posed therein. My consolation is that the theologians themselves seem essentially — indeed, manifestly — in the same predicament. And it may not matter too much how far out of one's depth one is if everyone has the same problem, namely seeing how near they can get towards the surface. For all the pontifications and pretensions of the specialists, there's little enough real difference between having one's head just hidden and lying full fathom five. Seen from above, in the light of reason, the only vista is the level unbroken expanse of personal nescience. Öd' und leer das Meer. And no doubt it's logical enough in its way that invisible things should be studied by invisible people. But wouldn't it honestly be better for all concerned and the world in general if they just stuck to a few simple basic predicates to which all can subscribe, such as good works, instead of exercising their brains and jaws on such

146

intractable and very likely nonsensical puzzles as — well, to take the first example that comes to hand and therefore to mind, the prime point you raise about whether one has to retain Christ as defining the difference between good and evil, no matter what the content of other religions may be. I can see that this seems entirely meaningful to you, and to Alan Race, and that the answer is 'yes' or 'no' as the case may be, which leaves me more convinced than ever that 'don't know' is the appropriate category. I can't even tell what the question means; it looks to me very like an empty vessel the main function of which is to be brimming and foaming with the heady wine of one's own opinion, which is then duly quaffed.

Still, I don't see why I should be excluded from these festivities; so here goes. The answer is this: 'yes' if you define good and evil solely or mainly in Christian terms and 'no' if you don't. As my ex-colleague in the Ministry of Labour became famous and rich for saying, 'it depends what you mean by . . .' etc. It would certainly be hard to deny that Christianity is (not just has been) violent imperialistic and exclusive. My Jewish friends are just as terrified by the cross as Dracula was. Not even Islam, try as it will, has unleashed such hellhounds. I don't see that these unlovable traits are much palliated by the fact that Jesus washed his disciples' feet. That sounds to me like Christianity washing its own hands. Besides, those same feet were hardly dry before the same Jesus was reported as saying 'no man cometh unto the Father but by me'. That's not in the least, surely, like a chap who says 'you're the only girl in the world for me'? It's a man who says 'I'm the only man in the world for you', meaning both this world and the notional and nebulous next.

It's good of you to say that my transmitter-receiver analogy helped this communication problem, but I certainly wouldn't see it as any kind of Christian formulation. We all use the telephone that works; but I bet Jesus wouldn't have seen himself as wearing an 'out of order' sign, or even 'emergency calls only'. He says, in the plainest possible terms, that he's the only telephone in the world that can give you a direct line. The minute that claim is objectively submitted to the pragmatic tests of the market-place and open competition, it is seen to fail. From the standpoint of all other religions, if there is anything of substance at all in their most deeply-felt and cherished beliefs about the nature of deity, the claim made by Jesus is not merely false but fraudulent (as the Jews have been pointing out for some 2000 years). As soon, therefore, as Christianity deigns to mingle with the mob, i.e. the rest of the world, and for that purpose steps down into the market-place, it will be accused, and with good cause, of hectoring not to say huckstering. If I were any kind of Christian, I should view dialogue with the gravest disquiet. It seems to me that Karl Rahner has omitted the fourth stage in his perhaps all too prophetic history of Christianity: first Judaistic, then Romano-European, then in dialogue with Islam, and finally non-existent. It's perfectly possible to fit the Terry Waite story into that sequence too; alas.

On that basis I can offer a comprehensive and (I think) rather compelling answer to your crunch question about how old chums can agree about works and not about faith — it's because those two have nothing whatever in common. 'Operational values' as you call them are surely social and intellectual, not specifically religious? Indeed I'd be prepared to argue that religion, as its history shows, is a powerfully anti-ethical force. Would the sum of human happiness and achievement in the Western world have been greater or less if Jesus had never lived? What other criteria of our *raisons d'etre* are there?

I don't mind agreeing, on the other hand, that human values would, if God existed, have something God-like about them. And, very well, if you insist, there's no apprehensible objective reality. But I must in my turn be allowed to say that the reason is solely our infinitesimally limited mental apparatus, not at all (as you seem to feel) that the universe itself is somehow basically confused. I agree in this context too that the fault is not in our stars, in any sense, but in ourselves. Then from both our standpoints, yes, I quite agree, there's nothing for it but to do the best we can as individuals, often in very difficult circumstances, to brighten the corner where we are according to our own lights, like so many fireflies. But the hope of thereby illuminating the obscurities of theology, or even seeing through glass slightly less darkly, strikes me as decidedly over-ambitious. God, I feel, is likely to remain above my head. So far as I know we've never exchanged any communication, telephonic or other. I shall just continue with my share of the proper studies until it's my turn for annihilation. Meanwhile I know of no objective formula for distinguishing between Christian theology and self-deluding folly, though I hope to remain open to approach and discussion on that point as on others. I've attended the course with all the patience and diligence I can muster (no doubt not enough of either) yet I can discern no spark of response to speak of: I infer that any rapport among those of differing faiths and non-faiths must be essentially humanist and secular; and I can't help further inferring that it is therefore in human as distinct from religious values that any such rapport resides. Ordinary experience tells me that religion, which by definition binds together certain ethnic or social categories, by that same act exerts a powerfully (and I would say malignantly) divisive influence and effect among larger categories. Wherever I look in history or the actual world, I see people killing or maiming or torturing each other in the name of strongly-held personal beliefs and opinions, not one of which is clothed in even the flimsiest fibre of objective evidence and many of which are nakedly insane; and this diposes me to wonder whether one's very first duty is not to abjure any such beliefs one already has and then to persuade others to abandone theirs.

It seems ironic, in such a frame of mind, to hear Christ claimed as a touchstone because he gave us a new commandment to love one another. But that wasn't new, was it? It's just plain Judaism, for a start and no doubt found in other faiths as well; it's among the many things, some of them very bizarre, that the Lord spake unto Moses, in Leviticus; 'thou shalt love thy neighbour as thyself'. I see what you mean about this commandment's incorporating a value so high that it equates with God, namely that it remains inconceivably remote from any human reality. But what, in practice, is the use of that?

All this is intended to be without prejudice to the values and delights of music, poetry, chess (and of course cricket) and so forth. But isn't it really rather apparent that these are all quite specifically *human* interests and activities — like love? Even when we subscribe, in all earnestness, 'with love, as ever', we still know, don't we, that the 'ever' part is, alas, something of an overstatement of the case?

> With love, as ever,
> yours E.

Otterbourne

February 18, 1987

My dear E,

Many thanks for your long last effort, signing off. So charmingly too. But I must not be beguiled. I shall cheat and award myself the last word.

With it, I say 'Bother! You still show yourself to be of an irredeemably(!) perverse cast of mind, though at one stage, round about Bultmann and Kierkegaard our viewpoints seemed to be converging. Then you go and shy away, back to fact and inference. And while you once said, e.g. Popper could not have invented the zip fastener, I retort in my turn, what symphony, what Shakespeare sonnet, ever saw the light of day via fact and inference?'

I must also strike a last Biblical blow on the source of loving your neighbour. I see you've been looking up Leviticus too (19: 18), in which case you can't fail to have noticed that the idea of loving your neighbour is introduced as a *subordinate clause*, in a long long passage mainly concerned with tribal and agricultural justice. "The wages of a hired servant shall not remain with you all night until the morning", and "You shall not let your cattle breed with a different kind". Now compare with any N.T. passage extolling the love commandment. But you can't. There *is* no comparison. Source the Leviticus passage may be: the full flower of meaning it is not.

Enough. By our different routes we find that theology does not solve everything — something to do with the wisdom of men being the foolishness of God and vice versa. So while you go back to action and your pile of books, I too have got my eye on a spot of praxis (*can* I have written praxis?) for when I get back.

> All love, as ever, Nancy.

150

NOTES

1. (p. 138) this is Nancy's inference but is not what I said. Alan Race.
2. (p. 139) So do I. Alan Race.

A BIBLIOGRAPHY

Barrett C.K.	*Essays on John*	SPCK	1982
Barrett C.K. (Ed.)	*The New Testament Backgound, Selected Documents*	SPCK	1957
Bornkamm, G.	*Paul*	Hodder & Stoughton	1971
Brown, Raymond	*The Community of the Beloved Disciple*	Geoffrey Chapman	1979
Brunner, Emil	*Revelation and Religion*		1947
Bultmann, Rudolf	*Jesus Christ and Mythology*	SCM	1958
Cadbury, J.H.	*The making of Luke/Acts*	Macmillan	1927
Charpentier, Etienne	*How to read the New Testament*	SCM	1981
Christensen, M.J.	*C.S. Lewis on Scripture*	Penguin	1980
Davies, Paul	*God and the New Physics*	Penguin	1986
Dodd, C.H.	*The fourth Gospel*	C.U.P.	1953
Drury, J.	*Tradition and Design in Luke's Gospel*	Darton, Longman & Todd	1976
	Early Christian Writings	Penguin	1982
Grant, R.M.	*Historical Introductions to the New Testament*	Fontana	1971
Gutierrez, G.	*A Theology of Liberation*	SCM	1974
	The Power of the Poor in History	SCM	1983
Hebblethwaite, Brian	*The Problems of Theology*	C.U.P.	1980
Hick, John	*Philosophy of Religion*	Prentice Hall	1963
Hick (Ed.)	*The Myth of God Incarnate*	SCM	1977
Hick and Hebblethwaite (Ed.)	*Christianity and Other Religions: Selected Readings*	Collins (Fount)	1980
Hooker M.	*Studying the New Testament*	Epworth	1979
Hooker M.	*Pauline pieces*	Epworth	1979
Houlden J.L.	*Patterns of Faith*	SCM	1977
Houlden J.L.	*Explorations in Theology 3*	SCM	1978
Houlden J.L.	*Connections*	SCM	1986
Hume, David	*Dialogues concerning natural religion*		1779
Johnson, Paul	*A History of Christianity*	Pelican	1984
Josephus, Flavius Tr. Whiston	*Collected Works*	Nimme	c.1870
Käsemann, Ernst	*The Testament of Jesus*	SCM	1968
Keneally T.	*Schindler's Ark*	Hodder & Stoughton	1982
Knitter, Paul	*No other name?*	SCM	1985

151

Painter, John	*John: Witness and Theologian*	SPCK	1975
Polkinghorne, J.C.	*The Quantum World*	Pelican	1986
Race, Alan	*Christians and Religious Pluralism*	SCM	1983
Ruether, Rosemary	*Sexism and God Talk*	SCM	1986
	To change the world	SCM	1981
Robinson, John	*Wrestling with Romans*	SCM	1979
Taylor, J.V.	*The Go-Between God*	SCM	1972
Taylor. J.V.	*A matter of life and death*	SCM	1986
Wand, J.W.C.	*The New Testament Letters*	O.U.P.	1946
Weil, Simone	*Selected passages,* quoted in Gateway to God (Ed.) Raper	Fontana	1974
Wiles, Maurice	*The making of Christian Doctrine*	C.U.P.	1967
Wiles, Maurice	*The re-making of Christian Doctrine*	SCM	1974
Wiles, Maurice	*Explorations in Theology 4*	SCM	1979
Young, Frances	*Can these dry bones live?*	SCM	1982
Ziesler, J.A.	*Pauline Christianity*	O.U.P.	1983